Cerrillos Adventure at the Bar T H Ranch

CERRILLOS ADVENTURE AT THE BAR T H RANCH

MAGGIE DAY TRIGG

Illustrations by Glenda F. Gloss

Sunstone Press
Santa Fe, New Mexico

ACKNOWLEDGEMENTS

To Henry, without whom it never would have happened.
To Fritz and Glenda who shared the experiences and without
whom it never would have been written.

First Edition

Printed in the United States of America

Library of Congress Cataloging in Publication Data:

Trigg, Maggie Day, 1913-
    Cerrillos adventure at the Bar T H Ranch.

    1. Trigg, Maggie Day, 1913-   . 2. Los Cerrillos
Region (N.M.)--Biography. 3. Bar T H Ranch (N.M.)
I. Title.
F804.L62T64   1985   978.9'56 [B]   85-9789
ISBN 0-86534-057-9

Published in 1985 by SUNSTONE PRESS
          Post Office Box 2321
          Santa Fe, NM 87504-2321 / USA

CONTENTS

FOREWORD

On February 14, 1847, one hundred years ago, Richard Green was born in Boone, Watage County, North Carolina. August 28, 1848, ninety-nine years ago, Mary Caroline Lewis was born in the same city.

There on October 31, 1867, eighty years ago, Richard and Mary Caroline were married in her old home. To this union, there were born thirteen children. Seven girls and six boys. The first five of the children, Clay, George, Calvin, Mae and Christopher were born in Boone, North Carolina.

Though by 1873, Father Green had a wife and five children, the call of the pioneer west was in his blood. North Carolina roots were hard to pull, but his desire to become a farmer caused him to "Go West". The journey westward was begun in 1873, though the family traveled no further than Jonesborough, Tennessee, where they remained two years. Nancy, the sixth child and second girl was born here on December 27, 1874.

To them, Tennessee was still "East", and the West being their destination, they proceeded on in 1875, the second leg of their journey to take them to Jacksboro, Texas. Here Father Green purchased 300 acres of farmland, built a home, and knew the thrill of being a farmer, having had great success with his crops and cattle. They remained here for ten years, raising five more children, Roy, Effie, Ella, Emma and Kittie. After ten years the family left Texas for New Mexico. On April 10, 1884 Mother and Father Green and eleven children started out on the journey that was to take them more than two months to complete. Four covered wagons, three of which were horsedrawn, and one drawn by oxen, along with 65 head of cattle, made the arduous journey.

The family arrived in San Pedro, New Mexico, without mishap, and here Father Green and the three older boys, using their large wagons, obtained a contract to haul ore from the mines in San Pedro to Los Cerrillos, where it was loaded on to railroad cars and shipped to the smelter in Socorro, New Mexico. This proved a profitable business, but, the lack of a school in San Pedro made the family decide to move to Los Cerrillos and establish a permanent home. Here in 1885, they purchased land and a seven-room house, which later became the Palace Hotel. This home was the birthplace of Richard, the last son, who was born in 1888.

Accustomed to working for himself, Father Green puchased the Madrid Coal Mines, which he worked for a number of years, until his health failing, he was advised to sell. The Colorado Iron and Fuel Company purchased the Mines and subsequently built the first railroad from Madrid to Los Cerrillos. It was after selling the mines that the plans for the hotel, which had been a dream, materialized. Their decision made, construction was started on the hotel in 1888.

The stone portion, consisting of twelve rooms, was erected first. Five dollars a day was the wage paid for an excellent stone mason. In 1890 native labor was hired to manufacture, by hand, adobe brick, and with this material the adobe addition was constructed. The approximate cost was $10,000.00

On the left, as you entered the building, the office was located. Father Green often played the role of "night clerk", so he occupied the little room directly in back of the office. The large room to the right of the entrance was leased to Mr. Julius Muralter for a tailor shop. His living quarters were in the back of the shop. Mr. Muralter boarded with Mother Green, and conducted his business for 22 years.

On the second floor, the room directly over the office, was known as the guest room or bridal chamber. A second bedroom was in back of this suite. Over the tailor shop were two rooms, occupied by Dr.F. Palmer, who was Los Cerrillos' only physcian. He also held the post of company doctor for the Atchison, Topeka & Santa Fe Railway Company. On the third floor there were three or four bedrooms.

The adobe addition contained a large room, used primarily as a dining room. It comfortably seated 32 people. On the north end, there was a large sitting room one of the most popular rooms in the building. It was furnished simply, but comfortably. It was here, gathered around the old-fashioned organ, that the family and guests spent many enjoyable times. South of the dining room, was a large pantry, from which a door opened into the front hall of the main building. Back of the pantry was the kitchen, and behind that, was Mother Green's room. It had a cheery fireplace, and made a haven for her to catch a five minute wink between her many chores.

Back of Mother Green's room was a small hallway leading into a bedroom reserved for hired help. There was also a large room used for storing purposes. The last room in this corridor was a bedroom, which was also equipped with a fireplace, and reached by a long porch. It was in this room that Ruth, the youngest and last child was born.

An outside stairway led to the second floor of the adobe

addition. Over the dining room was a large room, rented to the Masonic Lodge for a two-year period. Father Green was a member and became a 32nd degree Mason. Over the kitchen portion there was a long porch, off of which there were six bedrooms. In the extreme south portion there was a suite of two rooms occupied by Dr. Wm. Bishop D.D.S. who conducted his dental practice here. Dr. Bishop later passed away in this room.

When the room occupied by the Masonic Lodge was available upon expiration their lease, rather than renew, the room was subdivided and six additional bedrooms were made.

Throughout the years, there were several prominent people, who at one time or another occupied the "guest room". Of the most notable there was Thomas A. Edison, Ulysses S. Grant and Governor Prince. General Grant and Governor Prince were in Los Cerrillos to inspect placer mining locations. Mr. Edison was making experimental electrical research for an electric plant in Madrid. Only his colleagues and not Mrs. Edison accompanied him.

Col. Theodore Roosevelt, did not come to Los Cerrillos, but on July 4, 1899 the "Roosevelt Rough Riders" held their annual reunion in Las Vegas. Father and Mother Green, accompanied by Nancy, Effie, George and Dick, went to Las Vegas for the Fourth of July outing, and had the pleasure and honor of shaking hands with him, and of hearing him commend their son, Clay, who while assigned as Col. Roosevelt's Orderly of The Day, was killed in the first charge up San Juan Hill, in the Battle of Santigo de Cuba, on July 1, 1898. From this great man, praise was bestowed on the son, who gave his life for his country, by the simple gesture, and the words he spoke as he laid his hand on eleven year old Dick's head and said, "Dick, I sincerely hope you will grow up to be as fine a man as your brother Clay was."

The Palace, the Harkness and the Uptergrove were the big three of the hotel business. Then came the U.S. Post Office, a general store, a hardware store, 2 saloons, a bakery, a church and the inevitable "little red schoolhouse." These structures, and their founders and owners, put Los Cerrillos on the map. This writer is happy to know that 60 years hence, the old Palace will be restored to it's former status, to perhaps go down in history as one of the older buildings with a historical background and not fade into obscurity, only to be remembered as another "ghost town" of our great west.

Nancy Green McCleary
July 17, 1947

CHAPTER 1
NOW WHAT HAVE I DONE?

It was not until the late summer of 1946 that my life merged or rather, exploded into reality with the Bar T H Ranch and the Rock House, or Palace Hotel, if you prefer. Gunter, my husband, had accepted a one year assignment from the United States Department of State to return to post-war Germany to analyze, record and microfilm technical developments of the confiscated industries. Having no desire to spend that year alone, with two young children, I decided to rent our home in Redwood City, California and the children and I would join my brother, Henry, in New Mexico. Hopefully, my mother and father would spend much of their time out there, too.

I'd received many enchanting letters from Mother about the charm of the old Rock House, surrounded by magnificent century-old cottonwood trees, many accounts of the early history and romance of the Palace Hotel and Cerrillos, the beauty and fascination of the country — aptly named "The Land of Enchantment." The happiest days of my early life had been spent on a ranch so I envisioned a wonderful experience for my children. Gunter drove with us to New Mexico to await his orders from Washington there.

We made a stopover in Los Angeles to visit my sister, Libbie Allen and her family. Aside from not knowing how long it would be before I'd see her again, I needed her assurance that I was doing the right thing. Mother's letters to her had been as exciting as they had been to me and if my sister had any qualms or misgivings, she did not show them. Her encouragement was gratifying.

Our greatest worry was where was Henry? He was well aware of our plans yet we had not heard a word from him in weeks. He finally must have checked his post office box, picked up his ten day old mail, and realized we were on our way. He phoned us and we hastily scribbled his directions to the town of Cerrillos and the Palace Hotel.

"About thirty miles north of Albuquerque on the road to Santa Fe, you'll take the turn off to Madrid. It's Highway 10 and it'll be on your right side. The sign is kinda easy to miss so be on the lookout for it. It's a fair gravel road, a country road and at least you can't get off of it unless you try right hard. After you go thru Madrid, it's about three miles to Cerrillos then a few blocks farther on, you turn left and down at the end of the street is the old Rock House.

You can't miss it! Any idea when you'll be here? I'll sure be glad to see you!'' His enthusiasm was genuine; my anticipation was growing.

''You don't know how glad I'll be to see you, Henry! It's been a long time! Today's Saturday. We don't want to drive on Sunday and with two little kids we'll do more stopping than driving. Isn't there some place out there we can call you and give you and approximate idea when to expect us?'' I asked.

'''Fraid not. There's a phone in the general store but I doubt if they'd call me or deliver a message. Don't worry, though, if you leave Monday, you'll arrive late Tuesday afternoon. I'll hang around the house but if I'm not here, the front door won't be locked so go on in and make yourselves at home and I'll be there sometime.'' He answered blithely and that was that!

With bag and baggage for a year's stay, looking for all the world like the proverbial 'Okies,' we struck out in our secondhand 1940 Ford sedan. The back seat of the car was packed nearly to the top of the seats, but flat to make a bed for the kids, Fritz, seven and a half, and Glenda, six. We waited until the cool of the evening (air conditioning was an unheard of luxury) and started on our mad, all night dash across the California desert, stopping only long enough to grab an occasional bite to eat.

As we drove along, I thought back over the letters I had received and reviewed what little I knew about the ranch and the Palace Hotel which my mother had bought. I could understand my brother wanting a ranch. It had long been a dream of his.

When not in school, Henry spent his life on one or the other of the Trigg or Day family ranches. Both families had naturally expected that young Henry would follow in his father's footsteps and become a doctor and take over his father's practice. However, too much pioneer blood ran in young Henry's veins and too many years of the freedom of the vast open range had accumulated for his mind, body and soul to be confined between walls of office or hospital. By this time, however, the vast acres of both ranches had been divided, sold, redivided and resold. Henry had no choice but to find a ranch of his own.

He began his search of many years in Texas, New Mexico, California and even Old Mexico. Late one afternoon he was sadly returning to Fort Worth from New Mexico after another futile hunt. The road was steep and rough going. He coaxed his tired secondhand Chevrolet coupe up to the summit of the treacherous La Bajada grade, ease off the narrow road and turned off the protesting motor. He glanced toward the brooding Ortiz Mountains in the far distance, then gazed longingly at a vast tract of flat land sloping gently from its rugged peaks to the peaceful verdant Galisteo River Valley. After the recent and surprisingly good rains, it was green as he'd seldom ever seen New Mexico. The Galisteo River wandered lazily through that immense lush valley, so water would be plentiful, indeed as valuable as gold in this arid land.

As he stood there being gradually soothed by the peacful splendor of that nearly hundred mile vista, Henry realized that this was it. This was what he had been searching for. He became obsessed. He *had* to have that piece of land!

The particular tract Henry wanted was from an early Spanish land grant. In 1786 the Spanish Crown granted the Ortiz family the original tract of land. In succeeding years three owners had laid claim to the property, but the Atchison, Topeka and Santa Fe Railroad Company finally gained title after years of legal maneuvering.

The tract contained 17,350 acres; the price was right, twenty-six thousand dollars, and it could be bought. Henry got his ranch. He had already registered his brand, the Bar T H, (transposing his initials) and he had his bridle and saddle. His dream became a reality.

The property was bounded on the north by the Santa Fe Railroad, snaking along the adobe banks of the Galisteo River; on the south by the forboding Ortiz Mountain (although a good portion of the ranch staggered up its invincible sides); on the east by the Dolores Land Grant; and on the west by seven miles adjoining the Santo Domingo Indian Reservation.

On the northside of the property, nestled securely between the gentle hills and a sweeping curve of the Galisteo River, was an old, slightly dilapidated, dusty little town. It's adobe color allowed it to almost disappear, mirage-like, into the surrounding hills. What made it visible, in fact quite beautiful from a distance, was its oasis appearance, created by the abundance of large, old cottonwood trees which set it off from the surrounding adobe hills.

Los Cerrillos (pronounced ce-ri-yos) or "the Little Hills" was its name. The few squat adobe buildings were dominated on either end of town by much larger structures. To the east, the inevitable church and at the west end of town, all of three blocks, loomed an immense rock structure, gracious, yet forbidding, definitely run down, with extensive grounds, orchards and vineyards. This was the

Palace Hotel.

It was this building that caught and held my mother's attention. She and my father had come to Santa Fe after Henry found his ranch and got more or less settled. On each trip out to the ranch, she would beg Henry to drive her though Cerrillos. Although he tried to avoid doing this, it was not always possible and sooner or later he realized Mother would spot the FOR SALE sign in front of the once splendid, now dilapidated hotel. And it was as he had feared, she fell in love with the old stone building and promptly bought it, renaming it the "Rock House" and only added the word "Ranch" to appease family and friends. Thereafter both the Bar T H Ranch and Rock House Ranch were used interchangeably but as far as old-timers and history were concerned, the three-story building made from hand-hewn stone remained known as the "Palace Hotel" and so it is still called.!

Presumably by now Henry was reconciled to the house but I remembered a letter I had received from him shortly after Mother had seen that "For Sale" sign. It was more than just a letter, it was an urgent plea! He had written, "Maggie, you can do more with Mother than all the rest of us put together. Please, please try to persuade her not to buy that old bat's nest of a hotel in Cerrillos!"

Well, now I would be able to see for myself which one was right, Henry with his glum outlook or my mother who had written glowingly of her new purchase.

We had hoped to be in Albuquerque for a late lunch but the New Mexican sun was departing in a burst of magnificent color before we stopped for a bite of supper. If we'd had one lick of sense, we would have invaded the first tourist camp, (motels were practically nonexistent) but we were all determined to forge ahead. Gunter was re-reading the scribbled instructions and checking the road map while I was urging the kids to "Hurry up! Don't be such slow pokes. We still have a long way to go and I want to get there before it gets dark."

"Henry did say that Highway 10 was a 'fair gravel road' didn't he?" I nodded. "From the looks of this map, a very crooked, dot-dash makes it look like a country road, not maintained by the county." Gunter's tone was not encouraging. "Did he say how far it was from the turn off to Madrid?" I shook my head. He studied the map again. "I can't find one figure that indicates any distances except from here to Santa Fe. Here! You look!" He poked the map under

13

my nose.

I couldn't find any mileage figure either. "Well, does it really matter? We'll get there regardless of a number. The important thing is not to miss that turn off! Let's not forget to check our speedometer. Come on, kids. Let's get going or we'll never get there."

Twilight in the high Rocky Mountains is very short. It was almost dark when we left the little cafe. After about twenty-five miles we both unconciously began to search for that Highway 10 sign to Madrid; twenty-eight miles, and I was sitting on the edge of the seat; thirty miles and my nose was all but flattened against the windshield like a kid in front of a candy store. It was pitch dark. Our old fashioned, dust and bug-spattered headlights left much to be desired in the engulging darkness.

"Gunter, Henry didn't say from what point in Albuquerque the thirty miles would be. Do you suppose we've missed that sign? He did say it was easy to miss. Maybe you'd better start looking for a place to turn around." We were almost crawling along the two-lane highway. It was straight but narrow and no place to turn because of oncoming traffic. Finally, after what seemed like another ten miles, a side road turn off came into sight.

"Look Gunter, it's probably only a ranch road but at least you can turn around there." I pointed ahead.

At that moment we both spotted the sign. It was so welcome we forgave Henry for his miscalculations and our spirits soared as it was a hard surfaced road. But not for long! A few hundred feet beyond the cattle guard, as if strained beyond endurance, it abandoned itself to dirt, rocks and ruts. At least it was flat.

It seemed as if we'd been driving for hours. The last signs of civilization were that cattle guard, a few discarded beer and whiskey bottles and a plane beacon on a mountain top so far away that I would have sworn it was a star except for its unhurried change from red to white. I expected at least one cow or calf or horse would have had the decency to present itself. Suddenly a Stop sign loomed out of the blackness.

"Great day in the mountain" I exclaimed. "I wonder how few souls have braved this dot-dash road since Kit Carson's time! And a stop sign yet! Does someone out here have an over developed sense of humor or a surplus of stop signs?"

Neither! It should have been a Dead End sign. Not far beyond the sign the road came to an abrupt end and if we had not slowed down, we would have tangled with a barbed wire fence, gnarled entrana cactus and a lot of scrub cedar.

"My God" Gunter growled. "Where do we go now? Which direction? Can you see an arrow or a sign? Get the map out."

"Madrid can only be to the left and we should be about halfway there." I said.

What an optimist. More interminable miles through the pitch dark! The New Mexico sky with no moon has more stars than can be believed, but they shed no light on our little planet, and the mountain darkness was awe-inspiring — especially for city folks. Further, if the first half of that dot-dash road seemed determined to unbalance our mental security, the last half was hell-bent on destroying our physical safety! It swooped around sharp curves that plunged into deep arroyos. It struggled over scarred, rock-encrusted sides of sheer mountains to greater heights only to lurch madly over larger rocks and deeper ruts to new depths. It cerainly lived up to its history as the original stage coach road and seemed destined to defy man and beast. Finally we rounded a curve that could have been made only by run away coach teams and saw the first few scatterings of lights since leaving the highway. Another curve and the entire car seemed to settle down to a smooth purr as we reached the paved main street of Madrid. Thank God! The last eighteen miles had seemed more like one hundred and eighty. Another curve and the last thing on earth we ever expected to see loomed into the range of the headlights. Merry Christmas!?

A huge Merry Christmas sign careened crazily above and across the road. The black posts that at one time must have held the sign straight and proud, melted into the surrounding darkness and the unexpected greeting appeared to be suspended by irresponsible sky hooks. We could only gasp. No one had told us that Madrid had at one time been famous all over the country for its elaborate and authentic celebration of Christmas, including the Seven Signs of the Cross on the neighboring hills; and that every resident of the then prospering coal mining town was required to participate in the Christmas Pageant and have a lighted, decorated tree.

The kids had remained quiet during our adventure into stage coach trailing, perhaps as much out of fright as Gunter and I had, but now the Merry Christmas ignited their excitement which grew with every bump and curve. Presently a few more flickering lights, then that bridge. Cerrillos at last! There was hardly a kerosene lamp or candle fluttering along that two block stretch down to the end of the street. This exaggerated the feeling of desertion in the strange black stillness. Beyond the first block we began to see the outline of the huge house, silhouetted against the star-scattered sky. The enormous old cottonwood trees beside and behind it increased the illusion of size. Though I knew there were thirty-two rooms in this old hotel, as we drove closer I was completely unprepared for the increasing proportions of this mountain of stone.

"Any idea where the front door is, Maggie?" Gunter asked.

"Not anymore than you do, Honey," was all I could answer.

He drove straight ahead until an engulfing black void absorbed the light beams, clearly indicating there was a bluff beyond. He stopped under the cottonwood and turned off the motor and lights so our eyes could adjust to the inky blackness.

Finally, my eyes dilated enough for me to see a small ribbon of light dancing into the deserted street about forty feet ahead. The silence among us could have been cut with a knife. Not even my curious children showed a pretense of interest in joining me as I started to investigate that faint yellow strip. I picked my way toward it, praying that any rattlesnake in the area had already found his supper and was snug in a hole.

The screenless door was open. I peeked in. A smoking kerosene lamp fluttered on a rickety table and was surrounded by the remants of an unfinished meal. On the opposite wall, in a bent and twisted iron bed, were the bodies of two half clad children of undetermined age and sex. They seemed to have flung themselves across the unmade bed in a fit of fury, but sheer exhaustion had dulled them into a deep sleep. Henry had not mentioned two children. A mouse scurried across a corner of light. I retreated hastily, mumbling to myself: "Oh dear Lord! What have we gotten ourselves into?"

Gunter thoughtfully turned on the headlights as he saw me leaving that door much faster than I'd approached it. The light gave me the opportunity to briefly study the details of this mass of stone. Mother had written that the last owners had sadly neglected the house and in forty years had not improved it by one nail, board or stroke of paint but I was alarmed to see the precarious angle at which the balcony clung to the house listing dangerously starward. There were two doors in the shadow under its sagging boards.

Beyond the balcony, the tall bay windows, which extended to the top of the second floor, seemed suspended from the roof as the foundations had rotted or blown away years ago. I got back in the car.

"Gunter, those two doors can't be the front door so obviously this isn't the front of the house. Let's back up and go to the other side."

"Mommie, this house looks scary." piped Glenda. "Is this where we're going to live while Daddy is gone?"

"I think it looks fun," Fritz argued. "Do you think a real ghost lives here?"

Heaven forbid, I thought, but I wouldn't be one bit surprised!

I ignored Fritz' question. "Yes, my darling, this is going to be our home for a long time — until Daddy gets back." I was thinking that one year would seem more like ten. "It is scary only because it is strange and dark but it is up to us to make it 'fun'." I assured them though my words held less assurance for me.

Gunter backed around to the adjacent side of the house and again turned off the motor and lights. Then from the bowels of that total blackness we heard a ferocious barking. It would have awakened the dead!

"Henry!" I yelled. "Henry! Are you there?"

Making himself heard over the furious protests of his dog, he assured us, "Be right down. Gotta get a lamp. Come on in, the door's open."

Yes, it was open, wide open, without benefit of screen, crooked or otherwise, to protect us from the dark that oozed out as if to engulf us. I would not have entered that opening if I'd had to sleep upright in the car all night. We huddled in a clump waiting under the listing front balcony that gave the illusion of swaying in rhythm with the heavy vines that were clinging to it for support. From an incredible height in that inky hole, a circle of light began to spill toward us. In the middle of that patch of gold was the biggest, blackest, most ferocious looking dog I'd ever seen. I was ready to grab the kids and bolt for the car. But I was frozen in my tracks by the strangest sight yet in this incredibly strange night.

Henry! the pride of the family! So handsome in his white tie and tails as he had escorted his younger sister down the aisle when she made her debut. Henry! The closer he got, the more astonished and amused I got. Above his bare feet, he had on a pair of long, white, one piece underwear (union suits our Pappy used to call them) obviously four or five days in the wearing because of the bag in the knees. Above that, a face I could have sworn I'd never seen before, at least not under that tangle of uncut hair growing well over his ears and on to his unshaven face. And a full grown handlebar mustache yet! His grin of joy and relief at our ultimate arrival stretched his mustache beyond his cheeks and it disappeared into the darkness. Only the voice was familiar. We had not budged. I was too fascinated watching that apparition descend those steps and emerge from the darkness.

He motioned gently with his free hand and quietly commanded the dog, 'OK, Pot. You can be quiet now. This is your new family and you'll be taking care of them, too, for a long time. Go on and say hello to them.'' The upright bristles disappeared into his glossy black sleekness and his snarl, if one had any imagination, became a smile.

''Come on in.'' Henry urged. ''The door's unlocked.''

He had reached the hallway. Halfway between the upper and lower layer of that luxuriant growth of dark hair, I recognized a pair of eyes, smiling, beloved eyes. With a huge lunge, I landed in a one-armed bear hug, accompanied by sounds of giggles and laughter.

''Henry! you dirty, onery, good-for-nothing...you! It is you!'' I gasped.

More bear hugs, especially for Pot. He and the kids became instant and eternal friends. At this point my relief had reached the state of partial collapse, so I followed the lamp from the immense entry and hallway with the stairs disappearing into apparent infinity, (nineteen, I later counted) into the dining room-kitchen — my first introduction to the many oversized rooms with high ceilings and tall, thin windows with fourteen inch thick window sills. The high backed, hand carved oak Victorian chairs with spindly legs held together only by virtue of criss-crossed bailing wire, left great doubt in my mind as to their being a safe landing spot. I sat down on one, gingerly. It didn't collapse. I began to relax.

Henry had put the lamp on a very old, solid oak, oblong table and lit another one. The additional light aided my inventory of the room. It would have done credit to the best of Alfred Hitchcock, nay, better. It had an air of authenticity that Hollywood lacked. The far end of the room was dwarfed by a massive wood stove, set out at least a foot from the wall, flanked on the right side by a built-in cupboard and on the left was a door. Adjacent to the cupboard was a homemade flour chest and between that and the door we had entered was a magnificent quartersawn oak sideboard, boasting a beautiful beveled Belgian glass mirror. On the opposite wall was one of the house's ten outside doors. Butting up to this door was a homemade *something* that resembled a sink; a basin under one leaky faucet, a very small, rusty drainboard on each side.

"Mother wrote that you had no gas or electricity or plumbing but I'm glad to see we at least have water." I remarked.

"Water!" He scoffed. "Water! Yes! We'd have plenty of water if our master faucet was left on. But let's not talk about that tonight."

Glenda had an uncanny way of being on someone's lap and that someone quite unaware of how she got there. And there she was, sitting on Henry's lap and no longer able to contain her curiosity. "Henry, what is that thing under your nose?"

"Oh this, Honey?" he asked, gently stroking his mustache and twirling the ends. "It's my mustache. I'm cultivating it for the Santa Fe Fiesta. About five of us are having a contest. I'm a little behind but I sure hope I can catch up. Got a pretty good size bet on the best one. You'll get a chance to see the others before long."

"Can I touch it?" she politely asked.

"May I?" I corrected. I was ignored.

"Sure! It won't bite you. Only my teeth will." He gnashed his teeth together.

She giggled and patted it very gently. "It feels funny. How do you eat with it? Does it get mixed up with your food?"

"Oh, sometimes. But I just clean it off." he answered.

Lacking a pocket in his 'union suit' and seeing no paper napkin on the table, I expected him to wipe it with the back of his hand. Not so! He stuck his lower lip out over it, seemed to draw most of it into his mouth, then sucked long and loud. Glenda squealed with laughter. I almost got sick.

"Henry!" I admonished. He answered with a chuckle.

"Do you think I could grow one like that when I get big?" Glenda asked. We all chuckled.

While they were making friends, my eyes went to the light and the contents of the table: an empty bottle of milk and a box of Post Toasties.

"Is that," I pointed to the cereal box "all you had for supper, Henry?"

"Yes, and after riding fifty miles today on a darn broomy, a bronc at that, it tasted real good." He replied rather indignantly.

"Can I fix you something else?" Don't tell me you don't have a pot of beans stashed away somewhere."

"Oh, Pot Licker ate those. He rides with me all the time. He's my best cowhand and he was a lot hungrier than I was. Say, how 'bout showing you some of the rest of the house?" Henry changed the subject.

"Thanks Henry, but no thanks. Not tonight, if you don't mind. I think all of us have had just about as much excitement these last twenty-four hours, as we can take. How about finding a place for us to bed down and we'll see it *all* tomorrow."

"OK. I've cleaned out a couple of rooms upstairs. They're the only two connecting bedrooms in the place, so I figured they'd be best for you and the kids."

"Should we get the baggage first?" Gunter asked.

"Just what you need tonight." Henry answered. "No use bringin' it in in the dark. The porch light just burned out." He added with a grin. "It's just as safe in the car, maybe safer 'cause there isn't a lock on a door in the whole place."

"And you who use to be as scared of the dark as Mother and Dad..."

He interrupted, "That was before I got Pot. This place is safer than a fortress with him around. I don't think there's a human being except the family who could come inside this house without Pot takin' care of them. He even prowls all over this end of the house a coupla' times every night just to make sure that everything's OK."

"What about Fritz and Gle...?" My apprehension was evident.

"They'll be safer with him than anywhere on God's green earth. I've already told him once but maybe you didn't hear. Better tell him again. Come here Pot."

Pot came to him instantly, squatted on his haunches in front of Henry and looked intently into his face. "Come here Fritz." Glenda slid off his lap and they stood on each side of Henry with Pot in between. He patted Pot's head and very seriously said, "Pot, this is Fritz and this is Glenda. They are your family now and you are to take care of them just like you do me. No matter what they do to you, you are never to hurt them even if they hurt you. Understand? You and I play kinda' rough, but if they play rough with you, do not bite them. Understand?"

I could have sworn I saw Pot nod his head in understanding but maybe he just lowered his head to receive the kids' loving, trusting pats.

"What a dog, Henry! Where did you get him, and where on earth did you get that name for him?" Tired as we were, I could not contain my curiosity.

"It's a long story, Maggie. Sure you wouldn't like to hit the hay and I'll tell you later and..." Henry couldn't finish his sentence. The kids put up a wail

"Tell us now Henry." "We aren't tired. Please tell us tonight."

"W-E-L-L-L" He drawled. "It was when I was still living in Madrid. I was on the way home from Santa Fe and had stopped by Cerrillos to see my friend, Charlie Dominique. His dog had a litter of pups and they were old enough to be weaned so he asked me to take one of them up to Madrid and let if off on a side street somewhere safe so a child could come by and 'adopt' it. I picked out what I thought was the 'pick of the litter', stopped in Madrid near the school and let him off on a side street. I had to go up to the west side to check a tank and some fence so it was late before I got back to my little house which was the other side of town from where I'd let the pup out. Well, that crazy pup adopted ME! He was sitting on the door step waiting for me. I had a young kid working for me, and after supper he asked me if I wasn't going to feed the 'leetle doggie'. I didn't have any dog food — still don't have — so I fixed him some cream gravy in the old iron skillet, broke up some bread in it and set the pot on the floor. You should have seen him. He wagged his tail clear up to his ears lapping it up, every molecule! When we got ready to go to bed, I set him outside, smacked him on the rump and told him to go find a home with some kid. I guess he just sat there in the dark and waited till I got to sleep 'cause when I woke up the next morning he was in bed with me. Didn't have much for his breakfast so I fed him some of my Post Toasties, set him outside, smacked him on the rump and told him to go find another home. He was sitting right there on the door step when I got in that night and in bed with me the next morning and on the door step the third night. I'd even taken him back into the heart of Madrid, hoping some kid would take him home. Well, the third night while he was lapping up his bread and gravy, with a few leftover beans added, the kid looked down and said, 'Hendry (the locals here all pronounce

21

my name like it was spelled with a 'd') I theenk you got y'self a leetle doggie and your doggie's got a name, we call heem 'Pot Licker'."

The kids howled with delight and more pats. "Then what?" Glenda asked.

"That's all, folks." But the kids' disappointed 'Ohs and Ahs' prompted him to conclude, "Except he still eats just what I eat, usually from a pot, and sleeps with me every night."

"Speaking of night, it's LATE night so off to bed as fast as we can. Henry, you're the boss. Where to?" Gunter asked.

Henry handed Gunter a lamp, picked up the other one and headed for the stairs. We all traipsed after him like sleepy sheep, the kids automatically clasping the first available hand in the unfamiliar shadows left outside the ring of light from the lamps. On re-entering the main hall, I was again struck by the immense proportions. The place seemed endless in the flickering light, perhaps because the far end of the hall was not even visible. The fourteen foot high ceilings, the nineteen step stairway with its massive mahogany banister, all combined to give the place the impression of size beyond any reality.

As the weary troop started its ascent of that imposing stairway, Henry paused to remined us of the danger from the lamps, which, if dropped or broken, had both the fuel and the burning wick to start a fire.

The upstairs hall was as wide and as long as the downstairs one and as dark and foreboding. The only difference was that the second floor ceilings were only twelve feet high. Before we turned right into the room just at the top of the steps, we noticed another flight of stairs, not quite so high and wide, leading to another floor.

"Mein Gott, Henry!" Gunter exclaimed. "Doesn't this place ever end? It's enormous from the outside but even bigger on the inside!"

"Yeah! You've only seen a tiny portion of one wing and there are three wings. It'll take awhile to explore all of it." Henry said as he set his lamp down on an antique wash stand. "This is your room, Fritz and Glenda. Your Dad and Mom's is there." He pointed to a very large opening, the double doors fading into the shadows. After his remark about there not being a lock on a door in the whole place, I wondered if they would even close, not that it mattered.

He took the other lamp from Gunter and deposited it beyond that black hole amid remnants of his personal possessions. My travel-weary eyes slowly assessed the large room; the hugeness again emphasized by the flickering lamplight. Next to that bygone indispensable piece of furniture, the washstand, stood a chair of questionable stability. Across the room, another bent and rickety iron bed seemed to be attempting escape through the four small bay windows where it had been wedged with hardly an inch to spare on either side. Fortunately, the bed was longer than the bay and you did not have to risk life and limb crawling over its foot to get into it. There was not a curtain or covering of any kind to soften the black stare from those bay windows or the very tall, thin one on the opposite wall. Protection for a modest person? Forget it! I'd undress in the dark. I could not hide my expression of disbelief and Henry must have sensed my inward qualms.

"It's not much but it's all I can offer you." He softly apologized. "It isn't even very clean but I did sweep it before you came. With these winds out here it doesn't do much good to sweep. You can do just as well to leave the doors open and let it blow through."

I could have cried. Instead I buried my head on his chest and hugged him to keep from seeing just how close I was to tears. He returned my hug in a shy, embarrassed way, screwed a wry grin behind his mustache and continued.

"Remember how hard I tried to keep Mother from buying this old bat's nest?" I nodded. "I knew it was for sale. Found that out before I bought the ranch. And I also knew Mother's weakness for rock houses. Have you forgotten the rock house she and Dad built at the Rhome Ranch during the first World War?" I shook my head. "I made excuses as long as I could for not driving her out here to see this place, the 'For Sale' sign nailed on the balcony. Maybe if you had tried harder to persuade her not to buy it — God knows Dad tried..." He fell silent. "Guess it wouldn't have done much good anyway. You know Mother as well as I do and it looks like we're just stuck with it."

"Where do you get this 'we' stuff?" I was a bit indignant.

"Well, you've rented your house, to good tenants, I hope. They can be a real pain-in-the-you-know-what and you don't have much of anywhere else to go so you're probably gonna be stuck here till Gunter gets back and you can return to your safe, sane California life again."

Terrific, I thought. I grumbled, "Drat you! You could have at least warned me, given me so..."

"Why? What for?" He interrupted. "You might have changed

23

your mind and not..."

"Come out." I finished the sentence. "Yes, I would have come out under any circumstances. It's just...it's just" I stammered. "Well, I just wasn't prepared for this after Mother's letters."

"Mother's letters!" He laughed with more sarcasm than humor. "Mother's letters! You know how she exaggerates. Wait till you see the rest of it. At least we've been living in a few rooms in this part of the 'bat's nest' and have made some improvements. The rest has been deserted for years."

"The kids' bed is fresh, Maggie, but I've been sleeping in yours till you arrived. I'd better go round up some sheets for you." Henry was reaching for the lamp.

"Never mind Henry! I could sleep on a picket fence." I insisted.

As the kids were getting into bed, Fritz said, "Mommie, you don't have to read us a good night story. We've had enough stories for tonight."

"How about some extra kisses then? You certainly deserve them! You were the best two children, coming that long, long way and we are so proud of you and love you so very much!"

Pot Licker had made his rounds. All was safe and he had gone to bed; that bed being Henry's of course. But unbeknown to Pot, Henry's bed had been delegated to us. What a shock to see that huge black form stretched out full length with his head on MY pillow!

Henry grinned. "Come on Pot. We've been kicked out of our bed, we're now in residence across the hall."

With the agility of a gazelle, Pot lept over the foot of the bed and followed Henry and the lamp into the darkness. I mumbled aloud to myself, Thank goodness I don't have to get out of that bed the way Pot did.

Gunter, clad only in his underpants, had already twisted his long skinny body through the small opening and murmured an exhausted "Good night." By the time I checked on the children, judged the distance between the lamp and the slot at the end of the bed, blown out the lamp, peeled off most of my clothes and scrounged through that slot, he was sound asleep. Yes the sheets were sandy and gritty. Maybe we should have changed them. I soon learned that freshly laundered sheets acquired the same feeling overnight. There was something else in the atmosphere of New Mexico besides "Enchantment" — dust in the wind!

I was dog-tired yet my eyes would not stay closed; the galaxy of stars was a visual miracle but they could not close my mind to the events of the last few hours nor still the anxieties of the months that lay ahead...Finally I rationalized: go to sleep, you deserve it. No lunch boxes to pack, no school bus to meet, no commuter train to catch. You can sleep till noon so go to sleep! I did.

Sleep till noon? That was another citified luxury the "Land of Enchantment" does not condone. First, right after dawn it was the squawking of countless birds for their breakfast; then an army of flies with a vanguard of wasps descended through the open, unscreened windows. When the biggest, blackest of all the flies plopped right on the end of my freckled nose, I woke up with a jolt and the unpleasant sensation that I had not slept a wink all night and had no intention of being so rudely awakened. I pulled the covers over my head for protection against the marauders. But not for long. That New Mexican sun is hot the moment it casts its first fiery rays across a cloudless sky. It soon became a choice of annoyance beyond endurance — or suffocation.

CHAPTER 2
THE GRAND TOUR

The heavenly smell of coffee wafting up the hall and Henry's call, "Flapjacks comin' off. Come'n get 'em while they're hot!" delivered me from self-imposed suffocation.

Gas and electric ranges definitely have their advantages, but hot cakes cooked on top of an old wood stove are beyond compare. As is coffee boiled in an old enamel coffee pot and settled with an egg shell; but what Henry did to the "sow-belly", in cowboy vernacular, or salt pork I've never been able to find out or duplicate but I'm convinced that the stove had something to do with it.

After we had waded through stacks of those delicious flapjacks, Henry suggested that we have a tour of the place.

"Let me show you the bat's nest, or at least part of it," he said and added, "I'm sure Mother wrote you all about Mrs. Green who comes down here and tells her the whole history of this place. She insists that it was once a famous hotel, probably the most famous between Texas and California. Of course that was long before New Mexico became a state. It was Mrs. Green's family who started this place."

"Oh, then she is a daughter-in-law," I interjected. "I thought Mother said she was the last daughter living here but she must have been mistaken."

Henry shook his head. "No, you and Mother are right; she is the daughter. Her name is really Mrs. McCleary but nobody calls her that, I guess because her family had been here for so long and she is a widow. I think she is having a hard time of it and Mother offers her a bit of supper while she listens to her stories of the old days. Come on, follow me."

In one way, I was happy that we'd postponed the "Grand Tour" until daylight; we did not have to hold hands and stumble through a labyrinth of rooms by lamplight. However, in the bright sunlight, I wanted to cry out in anguish at the state of total depredation, to touch each maimed and crippled piece of furniture, to caress each scarred and broken wall. The farther we went, the more depressing the scene became.

The parlor was directly across the large entrance hall from the kitchen. The door was closed and I was hesitant to open it.

"Go on in, Maggie. You're holding up the tour," Henry had a mischievious grin beneath his broad mustache.

26

I opened the door slowly. On one wall was a potbellied stove boasting a black stove pipe big enough to exhaust the fumes from a medium sized industrial plant. A chair was leaning against the stove with its front propped on a TNT box in lieu of legs. Its seat was draped with the remnants of a tattered old pink bed spread which tried unsuccessfully to hide both bottom and box at the same time. Leaning against the wall in back of the chair was an exquisite gem of an antique table. Lacking a back leg, It was propped on a brick and its lovely black walnut top had been so abused that the edges had curled up in scorn. In the bay window, quite isolated as if it had been naughty and told to stand in a corner, was a lovely little pre-Victorian love bench. Its bottom had been boarded up solid (also with TNT boxes) and the arms held on with bailing wire. The meager substitute for springs and cushion was an undersized crib mattress. The remaining vacant fifteen inches were poorly camouflaged with wads of not-too-clean rags. An attempted cover up was the other half of the old pink bedspread. As least the color scheme was consistent!

Beyond all this, as if trying to hide behind the door, was one of the very few pieces of furniture in the entire house that had not been buried under countless layers of varnish. Its hard yellow pine had aged to the patina of polished amber. It was a tall secretary desk, obviously handmade, with leaded glass in the doors on the upper part and narrow drawers and cabinet doors on each side of a small kneehole opening.

"This is an interesting piece of furniture, Henry. At least I can tell what it is and what wood it is." I said.

"Well, it's a lot more interesting than just its appearance." Henry said. "Mother calls it the 'Thomas Edison Desk' because Mr. Edison himself used it as his desk during several of his visits here."

"Mr Edison! What was he working on while he was here?" Gunter asked in amazement.

"According to Mrs. Green, Edison was here at the Palace Hotel on five different occasions working on an electrolysis theory for processing gold." Henry explained. "He was hoping to perfect a method of mining gold without having to use any water because there is so little water available in this dry country. It has also been said that he was instrumental in getting Madrid to build a coal-burning generator for electricity. Part of the reason for the Madrid Christmas Pageant and the lighted Christmas trees in every home was to demonstrate the use of electricity.''

''That explains why they have electricity in Madrid and Cerrillos doesn't.'' Gunter reasoned.

''Yes'' Henry answered. ''But the people in Cerrillos were some of the first to hear his gramophone recordings. Again, according to legend, he made most of his 'broadcasts', if you'd call them that, from the balcony over the front entrance. Mother calls this the 'Edison Room' in spite of all the other historical events that have taken place here.''

''Henry, this place may be a wreck, but I can understand why Mother was so captivated.'' I admitted.

Henry remained noticeably silent as we started toward the adjoining room.

Gunter tried to open the door leading to the porch under that precariously hanging balcony. ''Gotta get a claw hammer to to open that one and a few others.'' Henry explained. ''I told you there wasn't a lock or a key to a door on the place and this one kept banging so I did the only thing I could think of — and I used the biggest nails I could find.''

We proceeded to the next room, a bedroom, which proudly displayed a bed with the typically high, elaborately carved walnut head and foot boards and the matching marble top dresser with a beveled glass mirror, truly an antique dealer's delight. Amazingly, every piece of furniture in this room was self-supporting.

''Why don't you use this room, Henry? It's ever so much more attractive than the ones upstairs and I would think much more convenient.''

''Coupla' good reasons, Maggie. This is Mother and Dad's room when they come out. Neither of them like those high stairs. And sleeping upstairs gives Pot more prowling room. He can check through the windows on three sides from up there.''

Next we went through the door that opened again into the wide hall. The upper end of the stairway was directly overhead and under the stairs was still another antique gem, the original hotel desk register. It too, was obviously handmade and it filled almost the entire space under the stairs. Scraps of leather buried beneath layers of dust indicated that it once must have had a beautiful hand-tooled leather top.

''This is another of Mother's favorite pieces of furniture.'' Henry boasted. ''You ought to hear her brag about it and she says she'd be willing to pay as much for the original register as she did for the whole place. Guess she's safe in saying that 'cause no doubt the book was destroyed or thrown away when the Palace Hotel was sold."

"Would be kind of interesting to see the old register though, because lots of famous people have stayed here. And that's a fact!"

On the other side of the door from the desk was an enormous armoire again handmade and covered with layers of black varnish. Henry patted it affectionately. "Mother's got a pretty good 'windy' about this one too." He grinned. "Seems a couple of fellows got into a shootin' fight in a poker game one night. One died on the spot but the other was just wounded and ran. Nobody could find him, not till he got to smelling, that is. He had hid in this closet and died."

"Mother and her stories! Where did she get them all in such a short time?"

"Most of them from Mrs. Green" Henry replied. "She comes down here two or three times a week and Mother really picks her brains. If the tales she tells aren't exactly true, they sure make good listening and Mother doesn't embellish them too much."

Henry gestured toward a door just across the hall. "Just another bedroom that I save for my Indian friends or a cowpoke if I'm lucky enough to have one. It's behind the kitchen and you can see it later."

He approached the door at the end of the hall. "When we go through this door, we are in the original wing of the house, built of adobe instead of stone. This is where the Green family first lived until they built the front addition, this old section then became Mrs. Green's famous dining room." Henry opened the door to usher us in but not before I noticed 'Dining Room' in elaborate gold and red etching on the glass transom above the wider than usual door.

"Oh dear God" I gasped as we entered. This was by far the worst yet! We stood stone-still and stared. The magnitude of this old fortress like room was accentuated by depressing gloom. Along the entirety of its sixty foot length, there were only two unusually small windows and only in the late afternoon would the sun penetrate the dingyness. Nor did the flimsy partitions, reaching part way to the ceiling, and the enormous collection of equipment, supplies and junk decrease its dimensions. Henry's saddles swung from ropes hanging from the ceiling and looped around the saddle horns, his bridles hung from nails protruding haphazardly from the walls, four or five sacks of grain and as many bales of hay, coils of barbed wire, kegs of nails and fence staples, boxes of undetermined content, every tool and piece of farm or ranch equipment that could be wedged through the door, clusters of questionable contents, and mounds of mysterious matter.

"I don't have a barn yet, Maggie." Henry apologized. "Haven't had time to build one. If I don't put all this stuff inside it sure won't be here in the morning. Worst part about it though, this is the closest way to the privy out back and there's a big hole where the floor's rotted out, so you gotta' be real careful."

We had slowly edged our way across the room. I stopped one step short of a black hole, a toothless, open mouth smirking at us.

"For the Lord's sake, let's cover it up!"

"Yeah, I've been lookin' 'round for a good stout board to cover it." Henry's tone clearly indicated that the subject was taken care of and therefore closed. I made a definite mental note that that hole had high priority on my MUST DO list.

We formed a single line, headed toward the far end of the strange partition and carefully wove our way through the obstacle course, and detoured the hole.

We reached the doorless opening on the far wall and made an about face, then retraced our steps back about twenty five feet though a wide hallway to a heavy, solid wood door on our right.

"What is this crazy hall for, Henry?"

"This was the passage way from the kitchen to the dining room and sort-of pantry. By the width of it, I imagine most of the dishes and tableware were stored in here. There's even a pass-through window right here." Henry pointed to an opening in the partition just opposite from the door we were about to enter.

"Mein gott!" Gunter exclaimed. "What a labyrinth! And you have to navigate this AND that lethal hole everytime you go to the outhouse? I think we could push this useless wall down." He seemed ready to start right then.

"No. Better not. Don't have any place to store the wood even if you could knock it down." Henry was evasive.

"In thirty two rooms you don't have a place to store that obstacle? What kind of an excuse is that?" I was a bit indignant.

"You haven't seen it all yet. Wait till you do, then you can judge." Henry pushed open the heavy old door, obviously the original outside door in the adobe building, we crossed an eighteen inch threshold and were in the third wing of the Palace Hotel, the last addition, and Mrs. Green's famous kitchen.

It was an enormous room, at least twenty feet wide and thirty feet long, with outdoor entrances on each side, one opening to the front of the house on the east, the other to the back door on the west. In the center of the floor was a rectangular section set with smooth, time-worn stones. The rest of the floor was covered with ancient pine planking, curling up against the stones.

"What is this, Henry? Why the stones in the middle of the floor?" Gunter asked.

"That's where Mrs. Green had her stove." Henry explained.

"In the middle of the room? Aren't stoves usually put against a wall?" Gunter asked.

"Not this one." Henry continued. "Mrs. Green cooked for a lot of people, a whole lot of people and there were always a lot of people bustling around in here, especially the Indians who helped her run the kitchen."

"Oh! Indians?" Glenda exclaimed. I wondered what was going through her vivid imagination.

"Yes, Indians, Honey." Henry ruffled her hair. "You see, Mrs. Green had only Indian help, here in the kitchen and in the hotel and they all slept around the stove for warmth, some say as many as twelve of them at once. Sure wish they'd left the stove. It's said to have been the biggest stove in this part of the country and everyone said it was a real dandy. Some swanky restaurant in Albuquerque bought it for pennies but they refused to sell it back.

"If it is big enough to cook for all those boarders, I don't want any part of it!"

"Tell us more about the Indians, please." Glenda begged.

"Well," he drawled, "her Indians all loved her, called her 'Mama Green' and so many wanted to work for her that the Chief had to use the 'merit system' in the pueblo to allow the Indians to live and work here. She was real good to them. Gave them a lot of free time so they could do their bead work and pottery and jewelry. They sold their wares to the passengers when the train stopped here. That's the way they made some of their money but she also paid them."

"But Mommie said the train doesn't stop here." Glenda said.

"Remember Honey, that was many, many years ago, maybe more than you can count..."

31

"I can count to a hundred." She bragged.

"OK, you win. but at that time Cerrillos was a big town and the railroad terminal was one of, if not *the* most important, in the whole southwest.

I had been taking a mental inventory of this room. It registered as dismal and depressing as the last, if not more so. At least the dining room housed some 'usables'; this room boasted only a vast assortment of useless, rusty, unidentifiable junk. Even a bonafide junk dealer would have been reluctant to cart it off. We had made our way through the litter and reached the door on the opposite wall. Henry pushed it open.

"This was Mrs. Green's bedroom and I think I have time to tell you one more interesting story about Mrs. Green's Indians, Glenda. They were her 'watchdogs', too and would have killed anyone who tried to harm her. Well, one night a man who Mrs. Green had refused to rent a room to, stole back later, pryed open one of the back windows and silently crept into her room without her Indians hearing him. He smacked a wad of cotton saturated with chloroform over her nose with murderous intent. One of the Indians was awakened by the strange odor, crawled to the door, saw what was happening and woke up his friends. That bad guy must have been purty' surprised when the Indians attacked him. They dragged him out, right then and there to kill him, sorta' quick like and get it all over with but Mrs. Green came to. She made her Indians turn him loose and wouldn't let them harm the man in any way." Henry concluded.

"But Henry, what happened to the bad guy?" Fritz asked.

"Now that's probably another good story if I only knew it, which I don't. You'll just have to use your own imagination, but I'll make you a pretty good wager he never returned to visit Mrs. Green again." Henry replied.

Mrs. Green's bedroom was not stuffed quite as full of rubble as the last two rooms. There was a brass bed, springs and mattress sagging of course, and several pieces of furniture well worth restoration. One detail I almost overlooked or didn't see because of the discards piled in front of it, a lovely little corner fireplace. It was boarded up with TNT boxing!

Gunter could no longer contain his curiostiy. "Herr Gott! Henry, where did all the TNT boxes come from? Was Mr. Green in the dynamite buisiness?"

"No. But I'll tell you about that later when I can show you at the same time." Henry replied.

The 'tour' continued through yet more seemingly endless and equally dilapidated, unused rooms, two quite large ones, two smaller, a long hallway and three outside doors. Little wonder Pot had to do a lot of prowling. We traced our way back to the abandoned kitchen and headed for the back door on the west side of the house.

"Better show you the 'Path' while we're this close. You may be needing it. Can't nail this door shut 'cause we have to use it but be damn sure you keep it closed at all times!" Henry looked sternly at Fritz and Glenda. "Wind and cold for one thing, but did you ever hear of mice and squirrels, snakes and rodents, even two-legged ones?" the kids nodded. "One of the most important laws of the land is that about gates or doors or anything that opens or closes. If you find it closed, be darn sure it's closed again after you've gone through. If it's open, leave it open!"

"Why is it so important to leave a gate open if you find it open?" Fritz inquired.

"Can a calf or a colt or a lamb open a gate?" Henry's tone was extremely patient as the kids shook their heads. "What happens to that little animal if its Mammy is on the other side of that closed gate?"

"O-o-o-h." They nodded their understanding.

He had opened another solid wood exterior door and pointed toward the privy, a leaning, dilapidated 'two-holer' that had seen its prime generations before. Its back was to the house, its sagging door opening toward the bitter west winds and a slowly dying orchard. The ceaseless wind had blown at least half of the earth away from the bottom. Little matter on a balmy, sunny summer day, but on a freezing, windy night, or during a snow storm?

"It looks like a tall, skinny playhouse, Henry. We had our own playhouse at home that Daddy built but it didn't look like this." Fritz said. "But why do you call it 'path'?"

Henry winked at me. Maybe he was even enjoying answering their questions. "When you have to use the toilet you find it in the bathroom, don't you?" Fritz nodded. "If you don't have a bathroom or a toilet indoors you have to use one like this outdoors, don't you?" He nodded again. "And you'll always find an outdoor toilet some distance from the house and at the end of a path. That's why

it's 'path instead of bath' comprende?"

"This ends the tour for now." Henry said. "I didn't tell you but I've postponed a very important broomie chase till you got here..."

"What's a broomie chase?" Fritz asked.

"A wild horse chase." Henry answered.

"Wild horse! You have real wild horses?" Glenda asked.

"Yes! Too many. So we round them up and keep them or sell them. But I'll tell you all about it later. Do you mind if we go in your car down to my camp where I'm going to meet the best broomie chasers in this part of the country?"

CHAPTER 3
SOME PLANS FOR THE FUTURE

We had not had time to unpack the car. Pot eyed it suspiciously. Where was he going to sit? In the front seat with three adults? In that builtup, bed-like thing in the back with two kids? He looked questioningly at Henry.

"Sorry Pot. You can't go today. I'm going to be chasing broomies and they are spooky enough without having a dog after them. So you stay home and take care of things around here. They're just going to run me down to camp and they'll be back in a little while." He reached down and patted Pot as if he was giving a wife a goodbye peck. Pot squatted on his haunches in the shade of the balcony. (When we returned, he was still in the same spot but had stretched out to wait.)

"Better let me drive. These roads aren't exactly highways. You'll get your turn driving back." Henry kidded Gunter.

We had barely left the house when Henry looked down at me with a mischievous twinkle in his violet eyes. "Maggie, before I start answering all the rest of your questions, how 'bout you answering one for me?"

"Sure. If I can. Shoot."

"I've lived out here for awhile now and I need to give a baile — that's a dance or a party. I've gone to a lot of 'em and now it's my turn to have one but I wanted to wait till you got here so you and Gunter could meet the neighbors and my friends. Do you think you could spruce up the parlor and kitchen some more and help me throw the kind of party Mother and Dad used to have in Westover Hills, except in the New Mexico style? I've already spotted the calf I want to butcher for the occasion." The twinkle in his eyes had turned serious.

I shuddered inwardly. 'Spruce up the parlor and kitchen some more?' 'a Westover Hills kind of party?' And before Gunter left and he was expecting his orders from the State Department within two weeks? I gulped silently to drown the butterflies that had suddenly lit in the middle of my solar plexus and covered my anxiety by joking, "Oh sure, Henry, a baile will be fun and I'm sure I can figure out a few ways to spruce things up if we don't run out of TNT boxes and if you aren't too particular." My mind was already forming the inevitable questions racing through my head.

"You look around the house today to see what you can find

that is usable and we'll talk about it when I get home tonight." As I fell silent, Henry sensed my concern. "I know that sounds like a pretty tall order. I've been trying to do some sprucing up myself. You should have seen the place when Mother and Dad first bought it. So anything you can do will be an improvement. And I hereby give you my full permission to do whatever you want." He grinned and that was that!

By now we had crossed the railroad tracks and the smooth, sandy river bed of the San Marcos Creek, dry as parchment although totally impassable during New Mexico's infamous flash floods. We began winding up one of the steepest, roughest roads a vehicle ever had to navigate. I strained to see where the ascent might possibly end. It didn't! It snaked its way around and up the edge of a massive rock monolith. The road was cut into the solid stone and was wide enough for one car only! Henry shifted into low gear and grinned as we lurched and bounced ever upward. "We'll make it. Haven't failed to yet. Only had to back down twice." He deftly avoided the deep ruts. "You were asking about the TNT boxes." He looked at Gunter.

"Are you trying to change the subject? What on earth do TNT boxes have to do with this gosh-awful road? This poor old car won't last long at this rate." I said, woefully.

"Well, this is Devil's Throne..." He ignored my protests.

"Aptly named!"

"Around the turn of the century, the Galisteo River went on an all time record rampage and washed out not only the road at the foot of this hunk of stone but it also washed out the main line of the Santa Fe Railroad. There was no suitable place to build a bridge across the river for the railroad so there was no choice except to blast another road bed. The charges of dynamite were so terrific that it did a lot of damage to Rock House. You'll see it when you get to looking around other parts of the place that we didn't get time to see this morning."

"For instance?" I asked.

"Most of the mirrors were shattered or cracked and I don't know how many window panes were broken."

"And the broken window panes still haven't been replaced after forty years?" Gunter was incredulous.

"Nope! And if they are going to get replaced, you know who is going to do it. But there's no hurry at this stage in the game, the damage has already been done, and a few more rains, if it ever does, won't do much more harm. But back to 'Devil's Throne'. They spent most of the money and TNT on the railroad and seemed to forget this, a much-needed, often traveled road..."

"Wh-a-a-t? This car-killer?" I interrupted.

"Yeah! It's the shortest road to the Indian Pueblos, to the main highway between Santa Fe and Albuquerque and to some of the neighboring ranches as well as the only road to camp. So something had to be done with what little remaining men, machinery and TNT they had. I guess this is the best they could do. You get used to it and it really isn't so bad except when it snows. Then it's a pretty good idea to take another road, even if you have to detour thirty or forty miles."

"So this is where all those TNT boxes came from." Gunter said.

"Yep!" Henry focused all his attention on the remaining part of the ascent, twisting skyward to a point where the road turned and disappeared. I dared not look backward.

The long, gentle slope on the down side looked like a super highway in comparison; it had even been possible to use a road grader on this section and two cars could pass without one of them being forced off into probable oblivion.

As we wound along the road we passed through two of the numerous former mining towns that dotted the area. Waldo and Old Waldo, remnants of the bygone mining boom, their adobe dwellings almost washed back into the adobe earth from whence they came. Only the stone foundations, a few derelict walls, and ruins still remained. We were so fascinated with Henry's narrative that I had all but forgotten the road. That is until we suddenly veered to the left and plunged into a deep gully hardly wide enough for a car to bounce and bump through.

"Are we still on the road, Henry?" Gunter asked.

"Actually, it's a dry arroyo, a creek bed made by the torrential rains. If we have slow, gentle rains, which we seldom do, the hard parched earth could absorb the moisture without this kind of damage. But when it comes down so hard that you can barely see your hand in front of you, it takes everything in its path. You should have seen this before I gave it a working over with a bulldozer. It's a pretty good road now." Henry defended. "This was the easiest access I could find to my dug-out."

He speeded up as fast as the poor car could lurch through the ruts, rocks and sand. I silently wondered if he'd taken up dirt racing and in our car yet!

"For getting stuck, this dry sand is much more treacherous than mud, Gunter. If your rear wheels get to spinning, they'll just bury themselves in the sand and about the only way you can get out is to get pulled out. So you've got to keep your momentum up and a steady speed and it's best to stay in high gear if you can." Henry instructed. He added, "But you might want to let Maggie drive home. She's probably had more experience driving in this crud than you have."

"I'll say!" Gunter seemed almost relieved as he replied. "I haven't had ANY experience in terrain like this. I'm more than glad to have her take the job. If nothing else, it'll eliminate arguments."

As our progress got slower and slower, I thought for sure the sand was going to thwart even Henry, but finally we reached hard dirt. We passed under the railroad trestle and up a sudden steep bank to a flat promontory overlooking a vast expanse of more sand, ending against a sheer adobe cliff in the far distance. Wandering lazily this way and that through this sand basin was a thin trickle of muddy water.

"There's the Galisteo!" Henry proclaimed as proudly as if it were Columbus declaring "There's the shore of America!"

"The Galisteo?" I sensed his pride and couldn't help teasing him a little. "That looks like someone forgot to turn the faucet off; it's a pretty skimpy creek!"

"Creek my foot. You won't think 'creek' if you ever see it on the rampage." Henry boasted. He surveyed the surrounding countryside. "Truck's not here yet but we'll wait for it here and they can take me across to camp. I could make it over OK but you might have some trouble getting through the quicksand coming back.

"Can we get out Daddy?" one of the kids asked.

"Sure. Be good to stretch your legs and run off some of your energy." Gunter assured them.

"Not so fast, kids." Henry admonished. "A few instructions before you take off. First, neither of you has a hat on but I guess you can't help that because you don't have one. It had better be the last time, though. The sun at this altitude is a lot more intense than you realize and sunstroke is more than a colorful term out here. Get your mom to buy you one when you get to Santa Fe. Second, don't get out of sight of this car and under no circumstances do you go close to that 'skimpy creek' as your mom calls it. It's full of quicksand pockets and only the instinct of a horse can sense and avoid them. And most important of all, stay away from the brush and rocky areas. This country is full of rattlesnakes, they come down here to water. They're very hard to see and can be hiding under anything for shade. Most times they'll rattle before they strike. Ever hear a rattler?''

Two grave nods. "Yes Henry." Fritz replied. "We had a big rattlesnake up under the oak tree where Daddy built our playhouse. We heard him rattle before Daddy shot him. And our white cat kept another one rattling while Daddy got his gun and shot him, too."

"I'm glad you know about them and just be careful of them at all times, comprende?" Henry warned.

"What's comprende?" Glenda asked.

"Guess you'll be learning some Spanish out here whether you want to or not. That's about all you'll hear except from the 'gringos'. It means understand or comprehend. Comprende, comprehend, they sound a lot alike, comprende?"

"I comprehende." Fritz smiled. He took his sister's hand and off they trotted, looking back occasionally to be sure they were still in sight of the car.

From this vantage point we could see across the mini-Sahara desert to the corrals and windmill at Henry's camp.

"See the door and window in the cliff just beyond the windmill? That's my 'dug-out;, my home until Mother bought that darn old 'bat's nest'." His voice had an unmistakable tone of disappointment. "I'd planned to build an adobe house above it but just as it is, it's a nifty little place and a whole lot better'n any of the line camps I ever stayed in at Uncle Dan's ranch in the Tucumcari Country."

"Do you stay down here often, Henry?" Gunter asked.

"Nope. Without Pot and me at the big house, especially Pot, Mother would be scared to death."

"Me too." I said. Then my thoughts returned to Henry's baile; how long will it take to plunder through all that junk to find any sprucing-ups?

My thoughts were interrupted by the arrival of a noisy truck conveying an extraordinary assortment of men, from a ten year old boy, to his grandpa, the 'old man' of broomie chasing, and a stock trailer fairly bulging with horseflesh. It was the Coleman family, neighbors to the west about 15 miles away. After a hasty introduction, they were ready to depart and Henry was wearing a happy grin.

"Wish you could go but I don't have another good horse. We're short one as it is, and I had to loan my other saddle to Bugger. Besides, you'd better stay home and watch those two kids. They'll be harder to keep up with than a herd of broomies, you can bet. Adios. See you for supper." He hopped on the fender and off they went.

As the dust settled and the quiet returned, Gunter and I looked at each other silently. We suddenly felt very small and isolated in the vastness of this rugged country. Our introduction to ranch life was so fast moving that I felt totally disoriented. It had only seemed moments ago that we left behind the order and security of Calfornia. We were both experiencing total culture shock.

The kids boisterous return restored some of our sense of reality. We all reboarded the Ford and headed for 'home'.

CHAPTER 4
THE FIRST SUPPER

A blind burro could not have crept more cautiously down the east side of Devil's Throne than I did on our return trip. Even the kids breathed a sigh of relief when we reached the bottom. A sincere compliment from Gunter was my greatest reward. My hands had stopped shaking by the time we reached the house. (No one noticed.) Several times, when the driving had not been too hazardous, 'ten days to spruce up' flooded my mind. Oh dear God! How could I live up to Henry's confidence and expectations. I could never refuse him. However, first things first and first was unloading the car.

"Well, but Mother..." Fritz objected.

"Don't you 'well, but Mother' me!" I gave him the WHAMMY LOOK! "The sooner we get this car unpacked and things put away the quicker we can start on our next adventure. Now get busy!"

I left no room for argument and sooner than I expected, there was some semblance of order and Grand Tour number two was under way.

"I wonder what is on the other side of this huge threshold?" Gunter asked. We were in our bedrooms on the second floor.

"One way to find out. You first." I responded.

Obviously that huge threshold, three feet wide, led to the rooms in the back of the second floor in the old adobe wing directly above Mrs. Green's Dining room. It had been partitioned into four bedrooms, two small center ones and a huge room on either end of a wide hall. The room on the north end had an outside door, (held closed by a hook and eye hasp,) which opened on to a rickety landing and a few remaining snaggle-tooth steps that could have been lethal if anyone tried to navigate them. Though sparsely furnished, these rooms at least, were tidy and useable. The house had been built long before the days of closets. Indeed, in those blissful days before income, sales and endless other taxes, the government's primary source of revenue had been property taxes, and in their straight forward method of taxation, buildings were taxed on the number of rooms rather than square footage. Since a closet was considered just another small room, prudent builders did not include closets in their building plans. Three rooms had a wardrobe or armoire in which to hang clothes.

41

Returning to the main hall, Fritz asked, "Can we go up these stairs?"

"Sure, you first this time."

We climbed the stairs to the third floor and the four medium sized rooms, each with quaint dormered windows allowing expansive views of the dusty town, neglected orchard, vineyard and garden and the magnificent vistas in every direction. Neither furnished nor tidy, the sole contents of these rooms were boxes of junk deliberately discarded by the last owners. It felt ghostly and deserted. We did not stay long.

At the bottom of the stairs was a door leading to the front balcony which, except for Henry's sporadic attempts with hammer and nails, would have been in immediate danger of complete collapse. We did not test it. Standing there, with the immensity of the place bearing down on me, I had the feeling it could have swallowed a small army and would surely need one to repair and maintain it.

"Mommie, I'm tired of all these dirty old rooms. Can Glenda and I go out and play?"

"Yes." Gunter answered. "Surely we've seen all of it. There can't be any more rooms."

"I hate to disappoint you, but we still haven't seen the upstairs portion of Mrs. Green's wing." I remarked.

"Oh no! How do we get up there?" Gunter grumbled.

These eight more medium sized rooms were accessible only by more, rickety, splintery ancient stairs climbing the south wall of the house. These rooms evoked the immediate impression that as soon as one room had been filled to capacity, the next room became the catchall for at least three generations of cast-offs and leftovers in various stages of disintegration. There were piles of this and that and a wild assortment of just about anything and everything. There were undoubtedly many treasures buried in the junk, but in that state, it was quite impossible to distinguish treasures from trash. My mood ranged from enthrallment to amusement, from apprehension to downright disgust.

I glanced at Gunter, my thoughts as disarrayed as the rooms we had inspected. He put his arms around me and pulled me close. "Liebchen, there's enough work in our wing to keep you busy till I return. Forget about this wing and don't even come back up here. It would depress a saint."

I held him tighter in appreciation for his understanding. The knowledge of the precious remaining days we had together overpowered my feelings of doubt and bewilderment.

Fritz and Glenda came in from inspecting the last of the rubble filled rooms. Their cry "Mommie, we're starving," shifted the mood.

But Old Mother Hubbard had nothing on Henry's cupboard. We did find a box of crackers, a half empty jar of peanut butter and a little jelly.

"While I'm clearing away one mess to make another, why don't you kids run down to the store, Zucals, and see if you can buy a bottle of milk and anything else you can find for supper. I'm not about to go to Santa Fe today unless I absolutely have to." I said.

I watched them run off, vibrant with the excitement and newness of this 'Land of Enchantment.'

Well, I thought, better get started on this mess. I tried the faucet. H M mmmm...two, no three drops. Not enough for a single spoon, let alone a dishpan of dirty dishes.

Soon the kids raced back. "Mrs. Zucal sold us some carrots and onions and potatoes. She said we don't have to keep them in an ice box and she's saving some meat in hers for our supper so you won't have to go to town," Fritz said with manly pride.

The kids were particularly delighted that the water was off, no dishwashing for the moment, and what else was there? They tore off with their newfound pal, Pot, in search of new adventures. They didn't have long to wait.

We followed shortly and paused to drink in the indescribable beauty of the golden hills, the picturesque adobe dwellings, and the vast turquoise sky. A rare moment of peace and calm and the rewarding feeling that this was indeed a magical spot, and that everything really would be OK. The kids were enthralled. My wonderful brother was here (at least somewhere within a fifty mile radius) and I would have *plenty* to keep me occupied while Gunter was away.

I recruited Gunter's help and we began a treasure hunt for useable objects from the trash piles. By late afternoon we had accumulated quite a number of odds and ends of chairs that could somehow be patched together for use at the *Grand Baile*, even if we had to resort to more bailing wire. I took a dim view of the TNT boxes! Later I would tackle the real restoration. But even now my list of necessities grew longer and longer.

"Ye Gods, Gunter! This looks like the list for a new bride

with a large dowry. What am I going to do?"

"You're always quipping at me, do the best that you can and that is all a mule can do." He smirked at me. "Guess you are going to be a mule in more ways than one."

If I hadn't been so tired I would have hurled something at him, but I resorted to a dirty look.

"Doesn't it seem to be getting awfully dark? It's only four or five o'clock isn't it?" Gunter asked. "In New Mexico it should remain light until eight o'clock in August."

We stepped outside the kitchen door and the entire eastern sky greeted us with the blackest, most villainous storm clouds I'd ever seen. Bulging and billowing, they threatened a Biblical deluge. Explosions of electric blue momentarily dissolved the blackness to be followed shortly by roars of thunder. It was then that we heard another roar, an ominous, continuous one that I had never heard before. The thought, 'where are the kids?' drove me toward that disquieting sound with apprehension. I rounded the corner of the house just as they came racing up.

"Daddy! Mommie! Come quick! The little creek...!"

They grabbed our hands and we all ran to investigate. The edge of the river was about one half mile south of the house and as we approached, the roar became so loud we had to yell to be heard above it.

"Daddy, it hasn't rained a drop here all day. Where did all that muddy water come from?" Fritz was astounded. So were we.

I shouted, "I think this is what you call a flash flood, Fritz. That's when a river is flooding from a downpour of a storm that's farther up the river." I pointed to the thunderheads to the east.

"It's scary, isn't it?" Glenda asked.

And so it was. At this point the Galisteo is about one fourth of a mile wide and what had been a muddy creek a few hours ago was a raging torrent from bank to bank. As we watched in fascination, Henry's fence, or gap washed out and the fence posts played a wild game of mumbly peg as they bounced in the fierce current. Henry's camp was on the other side; surely he wouldn't try to cross it. But I had something else to worry about. Feeding my brood!

Anyone with an ounce of intelligence would have started supper immediately, utilizing the last remnants of daylight. But knowing Henry's resourcefulness, I still hoped he'd find some way of getting home. And, quite frankly, the stove terrified me. I had hardly set the chimney on the kerosene lamp when there was a knock on the door. Pot raced to the door and his threatening growl left little to the imagination. I was very apprehensive. Would Pot mind me? Before I opened the door I patted him.

"Pot Licker, don't go charging out that door and biting somebody before we know who it is."

In the dim light I could not tell that Pot's bristling hackels had changed to tail wagging as he recognized the men, the first, tall, thin wrinkled; the other, the largest man I think I ever saw. Far from being strangers, they were obviously Pot's good friends.

"Is Hendry here?" the older of the two men asked me.

"No. He's chasing broomies." I hesitated. "But I'm expecting him any minute. He said he'd try to make it home for supper."

That was a mistake. I should have said simply 'no'. I could not refuse their request to wait for him. We performed a rather lopsided introduction, but the only name I could catch was 'Tiny'. It belonged to the giant, six foot six, around two hundred and fifty pounds. His freckles, face, hair and even the whites of his eyes all blended into various tones of sandy red, setting off the wedgewood blue of his eyes. Everyting about the skinny older man seemed too large for him. His work worn jacket hung from his skeletal shoulders, his pants from his hip bones and only his wide, protruding ears prevented his enormous black hat from sliding down over his face. His gaunt face accentuated his handle bar mustache. Could he be one of the contenders in Henry's mustache contest? Was Henry foolish enough to bet against that hairy growth that must surely have been cultivated for at least two generations?

They quietly took their seats in the far shadows of the room, Pot between them contentedly enjoying their attention. Their silent presence added considerably to my state of consternation. No doubt my greenhorn awkwardness with the facilities must have amused them almost beyond the point of control.

The first step toward supper was the stove. I was petrified. It had shown no signs of its peculiarities at breakfast; Henry was familiar with it and had learned to coax it into proper behavior. Had it been a bit larger, it could have served for the 'Cremation of Sam McGee'. At any rate, sometime in the past, someone must have gotten it that hot. The fire box was almost completely burned out and the gap between the metal fingers of the grate had no intention of accomodating an ordinary fire made from crumpled paper, kindling and small pieces of wood. they promptly disappeared into the ash box below, which was old and held together only by patches of rust. The oven door was sprung and no amount of slamming, banging, cursing, kicking or coaxing could induce it to fit into its designated place. But most annoying of all, the warped and curling surface plates seemed determined to smoke us out and trying to level a pan was a joke! If the fire was hot enough to tease a murmur from the teakettle, then you were forced to evacuate because of the belching smoke.

After three tries at cajoling a fire into life, I wedged a small log in the hollow grate and managed to start a smoke screen which rapidly absorbed the rest of the light from the dim lamp.

"Damn this thing!" I coughed. "Oh damn this...this belching Bertha!" The name stuck.

By now, the smoke and odor had penetrated the second floor. My long-legged husband came bounding down the stairs two at a time to see if the house was on fire. His relief was intense when he realized the source of the problem. Quickly, quietly and with a simple twist somewhere back of the stove he resolved the problem. It was almost like a movie film in reverse as the smoke retreated back into the stove.

"Dummy! Didn't anybody ever tell you about dampers?" He gasped.

"No!" I coughed. "The only wood stove I can remember was Granny's and she wouldn't let me touch it, not that I ever wanted to! How come you know so much about them?"

"We *do* have wood stoves in Germany!" Gunter said as he opened the door for fresh air.

That meal, when it finally arrived, was a study in paradox, a perfect example of a blushing bride's first attempt. Everything was scorched or burned almost beyond recognition, yet stone cold by the time I managed to get it on the table. The silent guests, and everyone else around the table, seemed hollow to their toes and for the life of me, I couldn't tell you what we had, probably because there was hardly a bite left over for me, let alone Pot.

The dishes we had managed to scrounge for supper were added to the pile from breakfast and lunch but I had forgotten to put water in the teakettle to heat. We had to stoke up the fire again with the last few gnarly sticks of cedar and wait for the kettle to fill from the trickle-dribble from that rusty faucet. I was on the verge of total

disintegration.

Fritz seemed to sense my state and asked, "Mommie, would it help if we went to bed without our bedtime story or should we help you with the dishes?"

His concern lifted my heart but I felt a lump growing in my throat. "It would be a *big* help if you two could tuck yourselves in tonight." I swallowed hard but the lump persisted and I shut my eyes tight to keep the tears from breaking loose as I hugged and kissed them both good night. Gunter took one of the smoking kerosene lamps and they headed upstairs.

I turned to face the sink. UGH!! Two feet high and not much wider and the drainboard draining everywhere but in the sink. Slowly I started the dishes, shifting from a stoop to a squat and back again. The lump in my throat had sunk to the pit of my stomach as pure hatred for the sink, the stove, the two silent, stony-faced observers, the circumstances, the blasted mess overwhelmed me.

Why were those two still hanging around? I glanced over at them and trying to keep the irritation out of my voice, said, "I'm sure Henry has decided to stay at camp tonight." They didn't budge! Surely anyone with an ounce of sensitivity would have left by now. They didn't expect me to put them up for the night? Or did they? Oh God! A shudder of fatigue, frustration and vexation gradually dissolved into silent mirth. Good thing too. The water was gone but the dishes were finished. Then my eyes caught sight of the dirty pots and pans still sitting on Belching Bertha. I quipped, "I'm sure I won't have to put a weight on those pots and pans. they're not going anywhere, but I am. To bed!"

That finally moved them, the 'show' was over, they shuffled out the door and I could finally giggle aloud. After all, life must get pretty dull and boring in this little ghost town. Could I really blame them for lingering on and on to watch this awkward tenderfoot?

CHAPTER 5
THE GRAN' BAILE

When that wonderful smell of brewing coffee aroused me to the first stage of consciousness the next morning, I was hoping that Henry had come home during the night. I reached an inquiring hand across the bed, hoping that Gunter's warm body would still be there; the spot was cold and empty. Disappointment matched my aggravation. We *had* to go to Santa Fe and I was faced with another unexpected responsibility, the trip to town. (I coined the word "cherrand," chore + errand as we drove to Santa Fe.)

The plaza and center of that sleepy, dusty town had changed little since the seventeenth century when it started growing along the banks of the Santa Fe river and the intersections of wilderness trails. Street signs were shunned as 'Modern Progress,' which was resisted in very conceivable way. Surely Santa Fe was the birth place of the "Land of Manana,' that tradition jealously guarded and maintained. Necessities had to be tracked down with the tenacity of a Sherlock Holmes. I wondered if I was still in the United States.

I was however, rewarded with two accidental strokes of good fortune; paper draperies, standard length only, for those fourteen foot ceilings, not stylish floor length, but at least they'd reach the window sills.

Then, in a musty, dusty upholstery shop I really lucked out; remnants and samples of tapestries, damasks, and even antique satins at ridiculously low prices as there was no demand for them.

Our return to Rock House was greeted by a rather sheepish-looking Henry. Supper was already started; a pressure cooker of beans happily cooking on the back of 'Belching Bertha.' We were all anxious to hear about Henry's adventures and the broomie chase, but our cavernous stomachs demanded priority.

"Don't put anything on the table except groceries or you won't be eating till midnight." I admonished as all hands started grabbing boxes and bags and bundles.

"Gosh, Maggie, you shouldn't have bought all this stuff." Henry apologized. "I have a lot of it in the pantry."

"Pantry? What pantry?" I pointed accusingly toward the bare cupboard.

"That's the cupboard. The pantry is down the hall. That's where I keep everything that doesn't have to be eaten in a day or so. You haven't found it yet?" He asked. I numbly shook my head.

"Com'on. I'll show you."

"It's so darn dark in this hall, no wonder I haven't found it." I grumbled.

It was large and very clean and the shelves that Henry had put in were well stocked. I burst out laughing. One shelf was half full of kerosene lamps, all in perfect condition, including polished chimneys.

"And I kept those poor kids grubbing through the dust and dirt and junk piles half the day searching for lamp parts that we could put together."

"I wondered why all that broken old junk was on the sideboard. Figured you were going in the antique lamp business; maybe make yourself enough to cover your expenses." Henry chuckled.

"Antique business my foot!" I retorted. "When I couldn't find but two lamps in the whole place, and they certainly wouldn't be enough for your Gran' Baile, I figured the only way I'd get any more was to combine and repair the junk! How did I know you had a closet full?"

By the time we returned to the kitchen, Gunter and the kids had unpacked the upholstery fabric and the paper draperies.

"Good Lord! This is better'n Christmas, Maggie!" He was carefully sorting through the lovely materials. "I'm going to be home for a coupla' days, so I can help. Say, I've never seen anything like these curtains. Are they paper?"

"Yep. But the price was right and I do remember hearing you mention 'sprucing up' didn't I? They won't last forever, but they'll be bettern' nothing."

He started chuckling. "They look nifty to me, and when they fall apart we can start a fire with them."

"Speaking of fire..." I was thinking of enough hot water for more than a 'spit bath.' I winked at Gunter and he slipped out to the car. At the top of our 'cherrand list' had been a tin tub. Gunter had hidden it in the trunk under an old blanket so Henry wouldn't see it: it was to be a 'presente' for him.

"Get out every pot and pan you can find and keep Bertha a-Belchin. There's gonna' be some baths around here if I have to wait till dawn for enough water!" The bucket brigade began.

Henry was home safe and sound, his broomie chase having been a great success. We had bought a bottle of wine to celebrate, and celebrate we did. In the warm glow from the kerosene lamps, and the friendly warmth contributed by 'Belching Bertha' we bathed, our first New Mexico 'bucket bath,' sipped wine and listened to Henry's exciting, sometimes frightening tales. This was, indeed the 'Wild West!' The kids were wide-eyed and silent except for occasional exclamations. It was well after midnight when, exhausted, *clean* and feeling close and content we all trudged up to bed.

After breakfast we showed Henry the 'loot' we had collected during the previous days treasure hunts. He was aghast when we ushered him into the room behind the kitchen. It was crammed with tables, chairs and even a lovely little love bench we'd found in Mrs. Green's wing, all assembled for 'operation spruce up.'

"Ye Gods, Maggie! You aren't going to try to fix *all* of these before the Baile, are you?" Henry queried.

"Who do you think I am, Houdini? No, you idiot! That'll take the better part of a year but they'll never get fixed if they're hiding out in almost three dozen rooms. We've got to sort the ones that can be fixed with the least amount of time and trouble for your Gran' Baile. Which reminds me, how much baling wire do you have on hand and where's the best place to look for TNT boxes?" I asked.

"I didn't know you knew how to upholster furniture, Maggie. Where'd you learn that trick?" Henry asked.

"Upholstering furniture was my Junior League Placement during the war. The Red Cross furnished the materials and paid the salary for a wonderful teacher who came all the way from Oakland. About eight of us worked from 10:00 a.m. till 4:00 p.m. once a week."

"Did you get paid for it?" Henry asked.

"Certainly not! That's what the Junior League is all about. That experience has been invaluable and it'll certainly come in handy now." I said, as Henry started setting chairs aside like he might cut a herd of cows. "Incidentally, how many people are you expecting? Have you invited everybody between Santa Fe and Albuquerque?"

"Not quite." He grinned. "But you never know who's coming or who else they'll bring along, plus the kids — and I mean all the kids. No such thing as a baby sitter in this part of the world so I guess there'll be a bunch of them."

That was all he said, and I figured that at that point my guess was as good as his. A few days later I got my first clue. A large calf was brought up to the lot to fatten before butchering.

The next few days were a frenzy. As each piece of restored, usable furniture came off the 'assembly line' it necessitated rearranging everything else. We moved more furniture than is usually stored in a warehouse. And it seemed that every guest Henry had invited RSVP'd in person (how else?) usually at meal time. But 'operation spruce up' was never long delayed. A thorough house cleaning had to be sandwiched in somehow and it seemed as if the dust and dirt, like the furniture, had been waiting for me, personally, for forty years. Oh! for a vacuum cleaner! If I could have just sucked it up instead of fanning it up in clouds that softly resettled as soon as I was beyond sweeping distance.

Thursday evening the 'fatted calf' was brought up for butchering. Good Lord! I thought. It's big enough to feed everyone in Santa Fe county! The preparations were almost ceremonial: every utensil scoured and scrubbed, buckets of scalding water in readiness, knives sharpened to razor edge. The block and tackle was hung from the lowest branch of the cottonwood tree in the back yard. We waited till the sun was setting to avoid the pestiferous flies. I waited in the house till the calf was shot, then quickly hauled up by its hind legs on the block and tackle and its throat cut for proper bleeding, and the skinning began with great expertise. Among other things, Henry was an excellent butcher. The kids observed in awe. In an incredilby short time, the last quarter was wrapped in the cleanest cloth and hung high in the tree to cool over night. It was the first time I'd seen 'back yard butchering' since my early childhood on the Day ranch. I complimented Henry. I thought the work was over. Little did I remember.

"Maggie, will you render out the manteka?" Henry asked.

"Manteka? What's manteka?"

"That's the leaf fat in the abdominal cavity, Dummy, and it has to be cooked over a very low fire." He explained.

Long after he was asleep I was still recovering fat from the most unpleasant part of an animal's anatomy. It was tedious and obnoxious; it also made excellent cooking fat and every drop was eventually used.

The day of the party, my *real* work began; baking the roasts which had been cut into about twenty pound chunks. That was my introduction into 'Belching Bertha's' intimate parts; her cantankerous top side couldn't hold a candle to her 'belly.' Wood, just the right size, had to be carefully positioned with steadfast consistency in her toothless grate.

Shortly before the guests were due to arrive, I made a final tour through the redecorated rooms. The transformation was miraculous and partly compensated for my backache. Candles and the old lamps, polished till they glistened, were placed in strategic places. The soft light was not only enchanting, it increased the illusion of splendor, and many a hasty camouflage job receded into the soft shadows. In lieu of flowers, I'd pruned the lacy asparargus plants that were going to seed and mixed them among the wild golden sunflowers from the yard. With a table centerpiece, laughingly dubbed 'the Weed and Seed original by Maggie,' the overall effect was close to elegant, as close as you could get under the circumstances.

As each new load of guests arrived, my efforts were rewarded with their praise; friends and newcomers alike were impressed. Fritz and Glenda took possession of the children, dozens of them. (Some of them *must* have been borrowed!) From the squeals and scampering from the upper floors, it could have been Halloween and they were all chasing, or being chased by real ghosts.

The live music arrived, three local residents with a violin, an accordian and a guitar. I had intended that they perform from the far corner, instead they grouped themselves in the most prominent place, presenting something of a hazard to the dancers. Little did it matter. The rough boards were just as hazardous and spurs were not allowed. The last box of cornmeal was sprinkled on the floor. It was going to be a 'Gran' affair for sure.

That evening was my introduction to the Shottish, the La Raspa and the Varsuviana. Everyone chose partners for these anything but subdued dances, even the children. Though I had ever so carefully swept the floor, clouds of dust from the inaccessible cracks mingled with powdered cornmeal and cigarette smoke and the air soon resembled a funky fog with figures frolicking in it.

All too soon I was summoned to serve the food. The guests' appetites matched their thirst and their zest for dancing. When children could hold out no longer, they trudged upstairs, located a bed that was not already occupied and slept through noise that would have wakened the dead. Each time the musicians would play a 'goodnight' song and reach for their instrument cases, the hat would be passed again. They paused only long enough to let the dust settle, wet their whistles and pocket their money. I was numb from exhaustion. It was 3:30 a.m. Would this party never end?

Not as far as the guests were concerned. A good party was as infrequent as a good rain! Everyone is loath to see either come to an end. But as a rainbow indicates the passing of a storm, the brilliant sunrise reminded the ranchers that the night had ended and cows still had to be fed and milked.

Early morning sunlight filtered through the dust as it settled behind the last departing guests, back seats loaded with half asleep children. We had a great decision to make: a few hours sleep or attack the holocaust now.

"I, for one, am too big a coward to face this debacle with a hangover — and that's all I'd have with just a few hours sleep. I'd rather work it off now." I volunteered.

"Not a bad idea, Maggie, where do we start?" Gunter asked.

"You're the engineer, Gunter." Henry added. "Maybe you'd better tell us where to start."

"Mein Gott!" Gunter exclaimed. "I'm a chemical engineer, not a domestic one."

"Well, let's start with the kitchen, it will take the most time," I said. Someone had to get the ball rolling.

Shortly after the 'Gran Baile' that dreaded summons from the U.S. State Department arrived. It was time for Gunter's final briefing in Washington before he started his assignment in Germany. Glenda and Fritz elected to say good-bye to their Father at Rock House. Though I tried to keep from looking as pitiful as I felt on the way to Albuquerque and at the airport, I was not so successful on the way home. The emptiness in my stomach was infinite; I could not contain the hot tears that ran down my cheeks. I did not realize then that our parting would turn out to be a permanent one for when he did return to this country, we separated and later were divorced.

There were many sleepless nights, worrying more about the children than myself — rattlesnakes, wild horses, dangerous cattle, unpredictable people, quicksand and flash floods. I finally had to come to terms with myself. I either packed up and moved back to California, even if it meant renting an apartment, or I stopped worrying! After all, this was the oldest place of civilization in North America and generations of children had somehow survived.

CHAPTER 6
"MACHINE PARTS"

In less than a week after Gunter departed, a phone call came through at the store, the message so urgent that Jimmie hurred down on his bike.

"Henry, Maggie, your mother just called. You are to return her call immediately."

Our beloved father was losing his battle with cancer; it was time to go to Fort Worth to be at his bedside. We left immediately.

Mother returned to Rock House with us the day after the funeral. The hours seemed shorter and the sadness less painful as we made plans for the future. The past was left in the past and we had challenging new reasons for sprucing up. We even discussed the possibilities of modern installations, especially since we were planning a family reunion.

"Yes, Mother, such things as plumbing, gas and electricity are very necessary, especially if you are going to spend more time out here, but it won't be possible to accomplish any of these things before Thanksgiving. Furthermore, they can't compare with the urgency of doing something about 'Belching Bertha'."

"Belching Bertha??" Mother asked. "Just who is Belching Bertha and what does she have to do with modern conveniences? Or are you just trying to change the subject?"

Mother's indignation was unchanged by the howls of laughter.

"I'm sorry Mother, we have christened that miserable old stove 'Belching Bertha; and before the rest of the family arrives we *have* to do something about her. Henry and I have priced new stoves and they are sky-high. So I guess we'll have to resort to finding stove parts."

A few days later, the 'cherrand' list longer than usual, off we went to Santa Fe, fully expecting to return with the trunk full of stove parts. After our previous shopping escapades, I should have known better. At the junk yards we were snickered at; at the hardware store, the salesman was indifferent, but finally he reluctantly filled out an order slip. After that there was nothing to do but wait!

The 'Scotch' in our ancestral blood was strong and frugalness was a matter of necessity. In a very short time, resourceful Mother had made a deal to buy our staple provisions wholesale at Charles Ilfeld Company. A working cattle ranch allowed us to get on the

'Entitled List' and provisions were hauled out in fifty or hundred pound sacks, canned goods in case lots and honey in a five gallon square drum. Henry's miscellaneous junk, feed bags, saddles and bales of hay were pushed aside in the old dining room to make room for the paraphenalia of the large (and growing) family. In a few weeks, additional space would have to be made for crates of lettuce, artichokes, celery and fruit that my sister and her husband were shipping from California as we prepared for the family to come.

Sally Haentjens, our youngest sister who lived in Pennsylvania, had had the alternative of coming to the funeral or visiting Mother later when she would be more needed; she chose the latter. A family conference resulted in the unanimous decision that the 'time of need' would be from Thanksgiving until Christmas.

The clan started gathering just before Thanksgiving, the Pennsylvania family arriving first, bag, baggage, baby sitter and boxes of secret goodies for Christmas. It's a wonder their car springs didn't break! What a joyous welcome! Sally was the 'baby' and we all adored her; her husband, Pete Haentjens, and their son, Peetie, almost two and the joy of our lives.

After the conversation had settled down to only two at a time, Pete informed us that he had to go to Denver on urgent business. He turned to me and grinned. "Want to come with us, Maggie?"

"Do I want to come with you! That's the stupidest question you ever asked!"

"Yeah, that was kinda' stupid. Ask Maggie if she wants to go somewhere and she's in the car before her suitcase is packed." He teased.

It was a short trip but fun. I had never been to Denver and the Brown Palace Hotel was like a 'Kings Castle' after the many months at our own Palace Hotel. I almost washed my freckles off in that luxurious abundance of hot water.

We returned late Wednesday afternoon just in time for a glorious sunset. In dreary, rainy Pennsylvania, such sunsets were almost unknown and it was doubly appreciated. The California contingent, Libbie (Mary Elizabeth, the oldest of the four of us) her husband, Roy Allen, and their five year old son, Roy III ('Little Roy') had arrived on the original Santa Fe Super Chief a few hours earlier, and Henry had met them in Lamy.

After our noisy, gleeful greetings had subsided to a dull roar,

Libbie pulled me aside for a quick whispered question, "Maggie, what machine parts did you order that had to be shipped in a huge wooden box and are so all-fired important that the station master won't release them without your signature?"

"Machine parts?" I questioned. "I have no idea, Libbie. We did order some stove parts, two months ago, that were supposed to be delivered three weeks ago and I'm gnashing my teeth to get them before the bottom of 'Belching Bertha' falls out and the whole house burns down. But you just got here. How do you know about the machine parts?"

"I made Henry stop by the station so I could send a telegram that we'd arrived safely. The station master showed us the box but wouldn't let us take it." She replied.

"I'm curious," I said. " Let's go up right now. Maybe he hasn't closed yet and it might be the stove parts.

Fortunately, he hadn't left but he did not extend the courtesy of a 'Hi' or 'Hello.' I said, "I hear you have a box here that I have to sign for before you'll release it."

He nodded and shoved a form across the counter but no pen or pencil. "Something to write with, please." I requested.

Grudgingly, he handed me a stubby pencil and while I was scribbling my name he asked, "What machine parts did you order, Maggie?"

I had no idea what was in the box and felt it was none of his business. I wished I'd had the courage to tell him so, but a small voice warned me not to antagonize him else he could cause real trouble. So I nonchalantly answered, "I'm not sure. We have to order so many things, stove parts, car parts, it could be either of those."

Libbie and I turned from the counter and headed for the box. He turned, too, but ducked inside his office. He had no intention of helping us with that monster. Searching for a clue as to its contents, I leaned over to read the sender's address, a name I'd never heard of, a street unknown, but it had been shipped from Ontario, California. I could have whooped like a Banshee for joy but didn't utter a sound. From the expression on my face, Lib knew instantly that it was something important. We had an awful time tugging and shoving it out to the car and if it hadn't been for the extra spurt of adrenalin caused by our excitement, I know we could not have lifted it into the trunk of the car.

"What in the world is in this box?" Libbie demanded.

"Well, I'm not sure, but if it is what I think it is, and *hope* it is, we're the luckiest people on earth!" I said.

"Don't be so mysterious, Maggie." She demanded. "Just what *do* you think it is?"

"You read the sender's address, Ontario, California. Doesn't that ring a bell or give you a clue?"

"No. The only people I know from Ontario are the Bianes and that sure isn't their name or address. And why would they be sending you machine parts?"

I gave her a mischievous look but did not answer. Then came the dawn. Her blue-gray eyes sparkled and she gave and excited, "O-O-O-o-h! Do you suppose...?"

"I'm hoping!" I interrupted. "We saw Jeanne and Philo before we left Calfornia and I asked Jeanne if there was any way we could make a trade. I'd send her turquoise in trade for some of the fine brandy that they produce in their marvelous winery. She told me that it would be impossible, that there were too many alcohol, resale and interstate shipping laws and that if either of us got caught, we could all go to jail. So I just forgot about it."

"Then it can't be brandy. Why did you get so excited?" Libbies's eyes had dulled.

My spirits would not be dashed. "Before Gunter left, Henry took us over to the Santo Domingo Indian Reservation and we stopped by Mike Leva's Trading Store. Mike had just received an unusually beautiful shipment of turquoise jewelry and he and Henry helped me pick out the very best pieces, a matched set of ring, bracelet and earrings. We mailed them to Jeanne the next day. So maybe, Libbie, just MAYBE! Keep your fingers crossed!"

We'd arrived at the house and I gave the horn three long blasts, the family's signal to 'come-a-runnin.' Pete and Henry were feeling the weight of that box and were groaning. Libbie joined in, complaining that we had had to put it in the car ourselves.

"You mean that you two pip-squeaks got this monster in the back of the car all by yourselves! I don't believe it!" Pete said.

"Well, we did! We couldn't do it again, I bet, but hurry and open it. Curiosity is killing this old cat." Libbie said.

"Reckon it's gold, Pete?" Henry asked. "It's as heavy as solid gold bricks."

The hammer didn't make a dent in opening the top. "Got a

crowbar, Henry?'' Roy asked. "You'll never get it open this way.''

We formed a circle around our treasure chest as if to protect it, chattering like magpies till Henry returned with the crowbar. Then we crowded so close he could hardly wield the handle. Finally the top was pried off. Twenty four (24) bottles of Assumption Abbey Brandy! The best of the famous Brookside Winery Brandies and all solidly packed in sawdust!

"Yep! It's gold alright!'' Roy exclaimed. "Liquid gold!''

Jeanne still cherishes her turquoise jewelry. I'll cherish forever the memories of that Assumption Abbey Brandy! We had many weeks of pleasure, many hours made warmer by the brandy's glow. After a freezing day's ride, Henry had always appreciated a steaming cup of coffee. Now, laced with a large shot of that fabulous brandy, it became a luxury.

CHAPTER 7
AN UNFORGETTABLE CHRISTMAS

The stove parts finally arrived and only six weeks late! Oh Happy Day! I was so excited I almost forgot to ask if anybody wanted to go into Santa Fe with me to pick them up.

"I think we should all go, including the children," suggested Henry.

"That's an excellent idea, children, and this will be my treat for lunch since 'Belching Bertha' has to cool down before she can be repaired," my mother, Nellie, offered.

We avoided a long wait at the S&W Cafe by having an early lunch, then we made a beeline for the hardware store. The stove parts box was so big and heavy that Pete and Henry strained to heave it into the trunk.

Thank heavens, Henry had Pete's engineering ability and physical strength to help him rebuild 'Belching Bertha.' It was almost lamp-lighting time before they were finished, and we were all grateful for the warm glow when the fire crackled within minutes — and without the dangerous dash of kerosene usually required to get her started.

Lib, the cautious one of the family, had merely grumbled about the warped top plates, the difficulty of keeping an even heat and the impossibility of using the oven. After wrestling with the oven door trying to cook the Thanksgiving roast, Henry had wired it closed to keep it from maiming someone. She was appalled when the snaggled-tooth fire grate was pried out in pieces. Who knows how many years since it had been in one piece or how many live coals had disappeared into the ash box that was never intended to be a fire box. It's bottom was precariously close to burning through.

"My God!" Lib gasped after thoroughly examining it. "If I had known this thing was in this condition, I wouldn't have spent one night in this house! And my room is right above it!"

"That's one reason why I get up before you do so I can empty it and you won't see it." Henry chuckled.

"And why do you think I've fussed and fumed every day?" I asked.

"Well, it's all right now, children," Nellie chirped. "We'll be able to have a turkey for Christmas dinner."

"I just wish we could get this midget-sized sink fixed in half a day." I grumbled. "I hate it almost more than 'Belching Bertha'."

"If we just tore it off the wall, do you think the boys would fix it Maggie?" Sally winked at me.

"You'd better not!" Henry threatened. "That's a whole remodeling job, not just a repair job, and you'd be in a terrible fix without it."

"When do we start remodeling?" Mother asked casually. "I've been very seriously considering moving the kitchen to Mrs. Green's original kitchen in the other wing of the house."

"Oh no! You can't be serious!" I moaned. "Traipse through the old dining room or outdoors to get to the kitchen!? Let's postpone even talking about remodeling until after the holidays."

The next morning, after the most superbly cooked hot cakes on 'Bertha's' new flat top (now that she no longer belched fire and smoke she became just plain 'Bertha') we explored some of the numerous places of this enchanting part of the world. We headed west on the typical 'washboard' road to the whistle stop on the main trunk of the Santa Fe Railroad near the Santo Domingo Pueblo, home of Mike Leva's famous Trading Post. Henry and I received his warm welcome, then with his infectious grin, Henry said, "Mike, this is the rest of my family, my other two sisters and their husbands..." Introductions were made all around. We were lured to the show cases loaded with magnificent jewelry.

"Maggie, is this where you bought the jewelry for Jeanne Biane in exchange for the brandy?" Libbie asked.

"Sure is. Is there anywhere else to buy Indian jewelry?" I asked.

While we were stalking and gawking, o-o-o-ohing and a-a-a-ahing, Henry had been quietly talking to Mike. "You haven't seen anything yet! Come here," Henry called to us.

We crowded into Mike's private little "cage" as he swung open the heavy door to his safe, his treasure chest for pawned jewelry. We were too flabbergasted for words. It was full of the most incredibly magnificent pieces of centuries-old ceremonial jewelry.

When we recovered from our awe and wonder, Roy, who was always searching for something rare and beautiful for Libbie asked, "Mike, how much does some of this jewelry cost? Could a poor man afford to buy a piece of it?"

Mike chuckled. "You could afford to buy it but I *can't* sell it. I am the Indian's banker and this is their collateral. Some of these pieces have been in the same family for generations and I never loan them one dollar more than they can afford to repay. You came at a good time. They've had to borrow money for spring planting but after the harvest and before their religious ceremonies, this safe will be almost empty." At random he handed each of us a piece and added, "Each of these pieces has strong spiritual significance for their owners."

Many of the pieces were worth thousands, a concho belt, each large, hand-hammered sterling silver, turquoise-studded medallion was laced on a leather belt, so heavy only a strong man could wear it without risking a backache. A squash blossom necklace of incredibly intricate design with countless, perfectly matched turquoise stones mounted in sterling silver; an equally exquisite matched set of necklace, ear and finger rings, and bracelet, each a priceless museum piece.

The Trading Post was filling with other people, sellers, traders, and buyers. We were sorry to see that heavy door lock away in cold darkness such unforgettable treasures.

Then on to the Santo Domingo Reservation a few miles beyond, where greeted us the waves and smiles from Henry's many friends as we slowly drove through the hand-swept adobe streets. Lazy swirls of smoke curled from the outdoor ovens as the daily bread was baking. An occasional animal skin was carefully hung in the sun for curing. The typical adobe Catholic Church looked inviting but Henry reminded us that time was running short. "Can't see it all in half a lifetime, much less half a week," he said.

The sun was reaching the horizon as we returned to Cerrillos. "This might be the best time to show you something interesting right here at home." Henry remarked as he turned right, crossed the railroad tracks and headed for the small hills overlooking Cerrillos. He stopped at the sagging gate that was supposed to offer protection for the grave stones of the popele who had once made Cerrillos a thriving mining town, most of them bearing a date in the 1880's. A few faded artificial flowers lay beneath a tilting headstone and bits of sunglow glass sparkled in the late sunshine. The winter chill chased away the sun's last warmth as we turned towards home.

The kitchen was warm and welcome and a pressure cooker full of beans whistled happily on 'Bertha.' Out came the lamps, the Assumption Abbey Brandy, then another all night vigil around the table to listen to fabulous tales, jokes and laughter and make sure the sun came up in the proper place at the proper time.

But alas, all good things, and the Haentjens vacation had come to an end; they'd promised to spend Christmas with Pete's family in Pennsylvania. All too soon, their car was packed and it was time for good-bys. But we couldn't find Henry! We yelled, we hollered, we whistled, we searched high and low. He had simply disappeared. Finally, with tears rolling down Sally's cheeks, they drove away. They could not have been far beyond the railroad over pass when Henry put in an appearance. Lib was indignant, Mother furious.

"Where have you been, Henry? You knew the children were leaving. they waited and waited and we looked everywhere for you!" Mother scolded.

"And Sally left here crying because she couldn't kiss you good-by. Where were you?" Libbie demanded.

"Aw, I had to go down to the pasture to see about a horse." Henry alibied.

"A horse! What's so important about a horse that it couldn't wait ten minutes!" I chided.

"An animal can't wait." He said gruffly, turned and stalked out. He hated being scolded more than he hated goodbys. I knew that was all the explanation we'd get.

School had closed for the holidays, Christmas eve was only two days away and the time was right. After an especially early breakfast, Henry told the kids, "Get your warmest clothes on. We're going to get our Christmas tree."

"Oh boy! Are we going to Santa Fe?" Little Roy's eyes sparkled.

"Who said anything about Santa Fe? We're going to get our Christmas tree right here on the ranch." Henry said matter-of-factly.

"But don't you just go to where they are selling trees and buy one?" Fritz asked.

"Oh no. We go up to the high country, find the prettiest one and chop it down. We have our own trees — lots of them." Henry explained.

Lib and I started for our jackets. "Who said anything to you gals? This trip is just for the kids." There was humorous twinkle in Henry's eyes. They were soon off in a scuffle of "Where are my mittens?" "That's *my* hat." and excited flurries and giggles.

They were hardly out of sight when the question of

decorating the tree came up. "Do you have any lights or ornaments or baubles out here, Maggie?" Lib asked.

"Are you kidding, Libbie? There isn't even one in the leftover junk boxes around here. Lights? Any idea were we could plug them in even if we had some. I guess we'll..."

"And you are not going to spend one cent on that kind of junk!" Mother interrupted emphatically.

"What did you have in mind, Nellie, real snow?" Lib asked.

"Don't either of you girls remember what we used for tree decorations when you were young?" Mother questioned.

"Well, if you two can't remember, I think I can," Roy piped up. "That is, if Nellie and I are on the same wave length. We did the same thing in Virginia when I was a little boy."

"All right, what's on your wave length, Roy?" Mother asked.

"Strings of popcorn and red cranberries. Do I go to the head of the class, Nellie?" Roy kept the smile from his mouth but not from the corners of his eyes. Nellie nodded with a satisfied smile.

"Oh, now I do remember." Lib said.

"But I don't remember ever stringing cranberries or popcorn, do you?" I asked.

"N-o-o-o!" She hesitated. "Sounds like a great idea, though but we'll need the ingredients. You wouldn't have any cranberries around would you Nellie?" Libbie grinned at Mother.

"Oh, not another trip to Santa Fe, I feel like a giant yo-yo constantly being pulled to and from Santa Fe." I moaned. "Let's check at Zucal's first. It's amazing what you can find there."

Zucal's saved us from being yanked by that yo-yo string. They had ordered extra cranberries for the season and found a box of popcorn on the back of a crowded shelf. We'd even rounded up three big needles and a ball of string before the tree cutters returned.

The kids popped the popcorn and strung each puffy kernel and sparkling red berry. They took turns looping the garlands among the branches. Finally, as we stood in slight awe admiring our combined creative efforts, we all acknowledged that it was one of the most beautiful trees we had ever had. One by one gifts appeared from strange hiding places, gifts and gifts and more gifts! How were we ever going to contain ourselves for two more days and not open them! The wrappings almost disintegrated from the kids rattling and shaking them.

Christmas day was glorious! The weather resembled balmy

Palm Springs, California more than a snow-covered mountain ranch. With 'Bertha's' contented glow and our excitement, windows and doors had to be opened. The big old kitchen soon became a colorful chaos of hastily ripped gift wrappings. Each of us had our own personal stack of treasures and the stacks grew higher and higher. The room was a hum of delightful cries of appreciation or surprise, thanks and wonder. Meanwhile the air was permeated with the aroma of our turkey and cornbread dressing, cooking in 'Bertha's' restored oven.

One of the most appreciated gifts was from Libbie to Henry. A large, round cake tin filled to its top with her homemade divinity, his all-time candy favorite. Not only did he not share it, he promptly disappeared and hid it in his bedroom. He was met with gales of laughter and mock accusations when he sheepishly returned empty-handed. It wasn't too long thereafter that Mother found that secret hiding place. She could not resist. As stealthily as a safecracker, she gouged a small opening in the crust, dug out a spoonful and carefully returned the crust. Henry forgot about his hidden treasure. Mother made daily raids. Weeks later Henry found his divinity. He brought it into the kitchen, this time intending to share. When he cut into the seemingly untouched crust with a pointed knife — poof! It just collapsed into a few remaining crumbs on the bottom.

Mother had been not only deft, she'd been thorough. Henry was entitled to his righteous indignation — utter disgust and disappointment. We could not contain our laughter. It was infectious. He finally grinned at his naughty, mischievous mother, ''Aw, Mother! I guess I'll just have to get Libbie to make me some more. And I'll darned sure eat it ALL when I open it.

The beautiful Christmas tree did not meet the sad demise of many other Christmas trees — a few ragtags of tinsel clinging to the brittle needles, waiting sadly beside overflowing garbage cans, for several mornings later we awakened to a world resting quietly under a white blanket. Hungry little birds looking for stray morsels of food were leaving telltale crisscrosses in the snow.

''Mommie, the little birds look so cold and hungry. I feel so sorry for them.'' Glenda was watching through the window. ''Can't we find something to feed them? I wish we could bring them all inside.''

''We can't bring them in the house, little pixie, but I've got a better idea." I answered. "You can share your Christmas tree with them."

"Oh no! Mommie!" She wailed. "We want to keep it forever."

"But the cranberries will spoil in this warm room, and the popcorn will get so dry that nothing will eat it." I assured her.

She was silent, thinking. Finally she answered, "Can we put it where we can see it?"

"Sure. Right in front of this window."

What a thing of joy that tree became. The children sat by the hour watching the little feathered creatures pecking first at the red, then at the white morsels. The birds chattered as happily as if it were already spring.

"When they've eaten it all can we make some more, Mommie?" asked my compassionate little Glenda.

"I'm sure we can, sweetheart. We'll make your Christmas tree last till spring," and I gave her a big hug.

CHAPTER 8
OPERATION RESTORATION

Mother was in Fort Worth on business in the spring of 1947 and heard that Henry and I were negotiating with Frank and Ruth Calvin to rent their ranch, stock and the seven bedroom rambling ranch house to be run as a dude ranch for paying guests. Nellie had a better idea. If Margaret Day and Henry wanted 'paying guests,' they'd be at Rock House was her response. 'Operation Restoration' became an obsession. Our after-supper, round-table discussions invariably led to plans, sketches, discussions and disagreements. One subject, however, was studiously avoided, Nellie's top priority, wallpapering the battered old walls. However, she bided her time.

Eventually, however, she casually mentioned, "Margaret Day, I think it would be wonderful if we covered some of the nail-pocked old walls." (With only two closets in the entire house, it seemed that whenever anything needed hanging up, out came a hammer and nail, usually the sixteen penny size.) "You can do everything and it should be very simple and easy for you to hang paper in the rooms we use the most."

"Oh Nellie!" I protested with stubborn disgust. "Flattery won't get you everything! I don't know how to hang wallpaper and I'm not going to learn. I'll putty up the nail holes and patch the broken plaster. I'll paint and restore the furniture or anything else I can but I will not hang wallpaper! Before you think of buying any you'd first better think of hiring yourself a paperhanger!"

"But Margaret Day..."

"Don't 'but Margaret Day' me. I'm tired and I'm going to bed and no more about *my* hanging wallpaper." I stalked upstairs.

Unbeknown to me, most of those unopened boxes Nellie had brought from Texas were filled with rolls and rolls of wallpaper. She was fairly itching to get them into production. Her anticipation had run wild and her common sense amuck with the stuff. Very inclined to be 'Penny wise and Pound foolish' she hadn't batted an eye at paying $250.00 for an original Hattie Carnegie dress or $75.00 for a Lily Dache hat but she'd spent tanks of gasoline running all over Fort Worth searching for bargains and close-outs of wallpapers. She had no conception of how many rolls it took to cover a wall, let alone a room, but if it was flowers, especially roses or pink and with a penny-on-the-dollar value, she bought it.

I'll never know how much scheming it took for Nellie to

persuade Henry to 'talk around' Cerrillos to find a paperhanger, but a few mornings later there was knock on the front door.

"Someone told me you are looking for a wallpaper hanger." The stranger announced.

"Oh dear, yes!" Nellie's eyes were sparkling. "Indeed I am! Do you hang wallpaper?"

"Yes Ma'am. Very good. I am Mr. Garcia and I'm the graveyard shift operator at the railroad station."

Negotiations were then made. "I work from midnight till eight, than I have my breakfast. We have our *comida*, main meal, about one in the afternoon, then I have my sleep. But I can work a few hours in the mornings and I like to be paid by the hour, not by the job."

This was not what Nellie had anticipated but she was desperate. I had refused to go near those unopened boxes. So a few hours work was better than nothing and his price was reasonable — or so it seemed. She had not reckoned that he might be tired after a long night at the station and well-steeped in the tradition of the 'Land of Manana.' He was slow and he was good but his only knowledge of cutting wallpaper was to measure a wall and whack. Eight foot patterns did not fit fourteen foot walls. His wastage was disasterous. My career as a paperhanger seemed inevitable. I soon learned that each roll did not begin with the same cut of paper and by alternating rolls I could save precious inches.

I began to save precious minutes, too, by cutting the paper then by brushing the paste on one strip while he was hanging another, and then by mixing the paste. It slowly dawned on me that invariably when the paste bucket reached the half way point, he'd calmly announce: "This is the last piece today. I go home to *comida.*" His *comida* time was not determined by the hands on the clock but, strangely enough, by the amount of paste in that bucket. I was too 'Scotch' to let that paste dry up and waste so I'd sort through the unused scraps and fill in the time consuming spaces around doors and windows.

Three rooms had been transformed from derelict to delight, then Mr. Garcia did not show up again! I had a sneaking suspicion that Nellie had told him that his services were no longer necessary. But I had served my apprenticeship and became the full time hanger for at least a dozen more rooms.

For the next three years, 'Operation Restoration' continued, but with sporadic and exasperating slowness aggravated by inexperience, incompetence and inconvenience. Each project was an exercise in 'why have it simple when you can have it hard.'' Priorities were established, and the installation of 'modern facilities,' at least water and bottled gas, were soon to become a reality.

Nellie had won the battle of moving the kitchen to Mrs. Green's original one, mainly for the convenience of having one door opening to the rolling stock on the east side of the house and one to the live stock on the west. Under the floor (that we'd hoped to salvage but which had come up in splinters) we uncovered an unexpected bonanza, a tiled drainpipe stretching the entire distance across the backyard to the bank of the San Marcos Creek. We also discovered a galvanized water pipe to the spot where once a windmill had stood. We could reactivate that later. But we dug in vain in hopes of finding at least one connecting pipe between the two wings of the house that would allow us to tie drainpipes together.

Nellie's secret scheme (if Henry and Margaret Day wanted paying guests) was to divide Rock House into six separate apartments and she had cleverly convinced us that, since plumbing and heating were being installed anyway, we should certainly have a bathroom on every floor. Deciding where to locate the bathrooms was relatively simple, three in our wing and two in the South wing, one above the other. Installing them, however, would prove more difficult. The solid rock walls were impenetrable, so the pipes would have to remain exposed; not a great problem as they could be disguised with paint and wallpaper. Getting water and gas in and connecting to the main drainpipe was, however, essential and there was no way to get those pipes through those walls. We had but one alternative, dig under the foundation.

After meticulous measurments and calculations, Henry marked the most convenient spot for connecting the pipes between the two wings. Excavating outside would be a cinch. But inside...? Under another torn up, rotting floor the earth was dry and turned to powdery dust under our shovels. It permeated every inch of the house and our sweating bodies. Soon the 'diggers' wore handkerchiefs as protective masks and everyone else abandoned the ship.

We dug, and dug and dug! Our anticipation grew in direct proporton to the growing pile of excavated earth. As the hole finally cleared the last foundation stone (it seemed as if we'd dug half way to China) we began our tunnel under the foundation and shovels were abandoned for trowels. We had been digging from each side, hoping the holes would meet. Henry's computations had been perfect. When metal scraped against metal there were wild whoops of joy!

Slowly the enlarged hole was filled with pipes; sewer pipes, water pipes, gas pipes. The indoor earth pile lay dormant, first watered down then covered with any available scrap of canvas, tarpaulin or even gunny sacks. The new kitchen held first priority. Being the painter, I insisted that it be painted before the linoleum or utilities were installed. Financial necessity demanded bargain basement prices on paint so once again I went rummaging in the Madrid General Store. I made a find and no wonder the price was right; it was a putrid color and had been sitting so long the paint had formed a solid block on the bottom of the can. I feared my arms would rotate out of their sockets before I could stir it into use.

The walls of the room we were converting into a kitchen were twelve feet high and to reach the ceiling I had to stand on the fifth step of the stepladder. I'd refused to play 'monkey on a string' up and down that ladder — continually moving the dumb thing — in order to paint the ceiling and walls of that enormous room.

"Henry, I've got to have some kind of scaffolding to paint that kitchen." I announced during breakfast one morning.

"Yeah! Guess it would help." He answered absentmindedly.

"Got any ideas?" I persisted.

"Scaffold. Scaffold." He repeated as if he was saying 'hocus-pocus' and expected it to suddenly just appear. "Yeah. I have a pretty good sawhorse in the wood shed. How high does it have to be?"

"At least as high as the fifth step on the ladder. Want to measure it?" I was making progress.

"OK. But let me finish my coffee, slave driver." He teased.

He got the sawhorse first. It was only a few inches shorter than the fifth step but I could manage the slant if I was very careful. As he headed for the wood pile I called out: "Don't come wagging in here with a 2 × 4. I'm not a tight rope walker and I already have a 'thing' about falling off ladders."

He was in his usual hurry and grabbed the first twelve foot board he uncovered. It was about ten feet long and would have been perfect — except!

A gallon can was too heavy for me to handle so I'd rigged up a two pound coffee can with a bailing wire handle. With great anticipations, I started the ceiling. I was standing on the ladder step and the make-shift bucket was on top of the ladder. When I was ready to move to the next area I stepped out on the scaffolding. There was a loud pop and I crashed to the floor, not knowing what had happened. I landed on my feet although it would have been far better if I'd fallen flat on my face. The sudden jolt had set the ladder in motion, swaying back and forth. With each forward sway, a slurp of paint landed squarely on my head! As if resenting my distaste of its color, the final lurch of the ladder sent can and all cascading down upon me. There was no way I could wipe the paint out of my eyes fast enough to keep it from blinding me. I tried frantically to wipe that obnoxious stuff out of my eyes, out of my hair and off my body before it dried and affixed itself permanently. Hours later, when I was regaining partial vision, I carefully examined the board Henry had brought me. Apparently *he* had not! It was a discard with a treacherous knot on the underside and about two feet from the end, exactly where I'd made my first step!

Dumb brother! I could have choked him!

The pipes slowly, laboriously climbed the walls. After the fourth contractor confirmed that the chimneys from the lovely fireplaces were unsafe, unusable, and unrepairable, due to the TNT blasts from Devils Throne years before, Nellie was finally convinced. So the butane pipes snaked their way into the fireplaces, and were eventually connected to shiny new stoves and we had heat in three rooms and two bathrooms.

Nellie would hardly let us finish one improvement before she was all fired up for the next one. The third floor offered exciting possibilities for a luxury apartment, perhaps for a famous painter or writer with a national reputation she thought. Time and neglect had really taken its toll; the dormer windows had to be replaced, repairing the mutilated walls was impossible and no amount of patching, painting or papering would suffice. Henry 'talked around' Cerrillos. Several days later Mr. Salazar arrived. "Yes, Ma'am, I'm a plasterer. A fast plasterer and a good one."

He was unusually tall, thin and boney, with an enormous mustache. We nicknamed him 'Mr. Bagote,' slang for 'Big Beard'. He was fast as lightning with his trowel and often the cement mixer, run by a rented generator, could not roll out the 'mud' as fast as he could slap it on.

Naturally, I was the 'sand boy' and could barely keep ahead of

71

the carnivorous appetite of that mixer. One day I didn't. I had always used the Jeep; it was simple matter of shoveling sand in the rear and our source was the San Marcos Creek bed, pure river-washed sand and better than any we could buy plus 'the price was right' (free) and it was close by. This day Henry was somewhere in the Jeep, my car was in the shop, so we had to take Nellie's Pontiac. The kids had loaded boxes in the trunk so it wouldn't get sandy. We drove to the same spot where I'd always gone in the Jeep. The kids helped load the boxes and we blithely got ready to start back to Rock House but the car got stuck, hopelessly stuck. The more I tried to move her, the deeper she dug herself into that soft, bottomless sand. Her belly was scraping bottom. We couldn't even pull the car out with the Jeep when Henry returned. That poor protesting Pontiac had to be dragged out with Henry's caterpillar and log chain. Henry kindly refrained from any sarcastic remarks but I would have agreed had he said: "Dumb sister! I could choke *her*!"

Mr. Bagote had finished the third floor. Nellie was enchanted with the transformation. It had dried the color of adobe and needed no further finishing. Nellie rehired him to splash his way down the length of the ceiling on the second floor hall, then the first floor hall, then to our dismay, the parlor. Dismay? It was far worse than that! Mr. Bagote refused to put his 'mud' over old wallpaper; it had to be removed down to the original plaster. We couldn't count the layers — just the blisters — and my miserable backache was becoming constant. This is one time I should have held out for paper, or perhaps I should say more paper over paper.

Thanks to bungling bureaucracy, electricity did not reach Cerrillos for several years after we'd started restoration. Fortunately, I was not at Rock House when it was installed! No way could wires be concealed within walls and ceilings and the poor electrician must have grown ulcers trying to hide them. The exposed wires I learned to tolerate but the those light bulbs swinging from the ceilings, never! I turned electrician.

The financial larder for restoration was almost bare so I haunted secondhand stores, junk stores, thrift shops and auction sales. My purchases were cheap thus the wiring was either lethal or nonexistent. After about the fifth battered up old lamp I lugged in for Pete to repair (the Haentjens were visiting us) he lost his patience.

"Damn it, Maggie! If you persist in dragging this junk home, *you* learn to repair it! Sit down! I'll show you how to do it and if you can't learn to repair and rewire it, don't bring it to me!" Pete growled. I learned. I managed to camouflage many of the dangling light bulbs except on the third floor. It wasn't important. That 'famous artist' had not found us and it remained unoccupied.

On one of her infrequent trips to Fort Worth, Nellie noticed that the Texas Hotel was undergoing some refurbishing. Among other things, new carpeting was being installed. Nellie bargained with the manager, a long-time friend, for the old carpeting. The price was right but the freight cost horrendous! And when it finally arrived at Rock House, the burly truck drivers stood fast to their union rule: they did *not* have to deposit it inside the house. They unceremoniously dumped the huge roll in the side yard, far away from the protection of the balcony. Its precarious location produced an often prayed for miracle in that desert-dry area, rain!

"Margaret Day! Margaret Day!" Nellie hollered. "We've got to move the carpet. It's raining and it'll be ruined!"

"Are you kidding, Nellie! I am not Houdini, though most of the time I think you think I am. It'll take four men and a boy to move that monster."

"Let's roll it under the balcony." She persisted. "I simply can not afford to have it ruined!"

But it was unmovable.

"I'll try to find some tarps or plastic or something to cover it." I volunteered. My search was futile but my effort at least satisfied her. We would have to wait for help.

Henry was spending most of his time riding the ranch. He was having a tough time finding some of his best cows and strongly suspected rustling. Riding in the rain was sheer joy to him so he did not hurry and it was almost dark before he came in. He was hardly inside the door before Nellie started barking commands. "You *have* do do something!"

"But Mother." He argued. "The minute I move it out of the rain it'll stop raining and a good rain right now is worth more to me than all the carpets in the whole hotel — old or new."

"If you won't move it, go find something to cover it up. Margaret Day looked but couldn't find a thing." Nellie insisted.

"Did you look in the woodshed, Maggie? I think there's a good tarp out there." Henry said.

"Even if I'd known there was one out there, I wouldn't have looked. It's too good a hiding place for rattlesnakes." I said. "*You* go look!''

"Gimme a flashlight then." He said. It would be totally dark in there and my mention of rattlesnakes did make him exercise a bit of caution. He found the tarp, the rain continued and everyone was satisfied.

It didn't even take too long for the outside edges of the carpet to dry for the tarp hadn't been big enough to cover all of it. Then I began to have an uncomfortable premonition. Who was going to lay that carpet? Three guesses! It took me four times longer to get that heavy, unwieldy carpet measured and cut than it did for it to dry. The installation was worse! But the hardest of all was the hand sewing! I'm convinced that was an early invitation for arthritis in my hands; my back had already succumbed. Eventually, however, the parlor was restored to its former elegance and footsteps no longer echoed down the long front hall.

Ater what seemed interminable months, the plumbing was finally finished. And joy of joys, the sound of water gurgled through the pipes! Henry's 'talking to' the higher-ups in the Atchison, Topeka and Santa Fe Railroad Company had resulted in a more constant, though never large, flow of water. The bathtub was slowly filling with hot water. It was unamimously agreed that to celebrate this great event I should have the first bath to christen the tub.

I knew it wouldn't be a long, leisurely soak-bath. Dr. Chris Mansel and his friend, Brian White from Lubbock, Texas had deserted their wives and children to come to the Bar T H for the weekend. To Chris, this was his 'never-never-land' and he came as often as his medical practice allowed. They had business in Santa Fe but whatever it was, they had not detoured the La Fonda Bar. They returned long before they were expected and were 'feeling no pain'.

"Where's Maggie?" Chris yelled as he came though the door. "I've got a present for her!" He brandished a bottle of my favorite bourbon over his head as if it was a triumphant battle flag.

In her young innocence, Glenda proudly and promptly answered: "Mommie is having the *first* bath in Rock House!"

I heard them coming. The shower curtain had been pulled so I felt safe and secure but just to be safer, I doubled up, jackknife fashion and all they could see of my skinny body were shin bones and back. Sure enough! Back went the curtain with a mighty flourish and both Chris and bourbon bottle almost joined me in the tub. Brian was close behind Chris. Nellie brought up the rear.

"Get out of here, you two!" She yelled at the top of her voice. "Margaret Day is taking a bath and you get right out of here!"

As far as they were concerned, Nellie's admonishments made the scene all the more entertaining. Henry was awakened from his nap across the hall and all the laughing and hollering brought him on the double. Fritz and Glenda crowded in.

A kitchen broom was hanging on a nail behind the door. As a last resort, Nellie grabbed it. When her efforts at sweeping the intruders out failed, she used the handle. A couple of well-aimed whacks brought howls and retreat. I finished my bath with a chuckle. This tub sure got a social christenting, I thought but wasn't that typical of most things at the Bar T H?

CHAPTER 9
A FAMILY GHOST

Nellie had invited a number of guests for a Fourth of July house party and had managed to wheedle me into agreeing to restore four more bedrooms, those on the second floor of the old adobe wing directly behind our wing of the house.

"Yes, Nellie, I got the wallpaper paste. You didn't add it to the 'cherrand list' but I didn't forget. I know how anxious you are to get those other rooms restored before you have your party. Say, do you have any idea by now how many there'll be?" I asked. "No! Don't answer that. The shock might kill me and nothing will get finished." I added.

"I'm not sure how many will come and won't know till we count heads at the table. But I don't want you to kill yourself. Just do the best you can." Nellie said.

It was a short week but long hours. After the big room on the south end was finished, the two smaller adjoining rooms were much easier. I had plenty of paper, for a change, and my supplies were already upstairs.

I surveyed the last room, the corner room with the separate entrance and outdoor steps. I was tired. After the countless trips up and down that ladder I felt like a two-legged spider in an oversized web. It would be a herculean task and I was no Hercules; far from it. Just a wiry, half-skinny bundle of energy and determination in my early thirties but with the increasing 'miseries' in my back, feeling more like one hundred and thirty.

"Wouldn't it take a lot less time just to clean and paint it?" Nellie coaxed.

"Oh, Mother, it's the worst one yet. Almost all the windows were broken and it got the rains from both directions. I don't care how many coats of paint I slap on it, it'll still look terrible."

"You'd be finished sooner and I can see you're tired."

She was right so I ended up painting it. It looked terrible and I hated it. I never went into that room unless I absolutely had to.

Nellie sensed my aversion and tried to distract my attention from the paint brush. "Margaret Day, I know you don't like this room but according to Mrs. Green, it's one of the most interesting ones in the whole house..."

"I have the feeling I'm about to hear a story." I interrupted.

"You remember, this whole floor was the first Masonic

Lodge in New Mexico. That's the reason for the outside steps,'' Nellie continued. "After it was partitioned, Lew Wallace —''

"Lew Wallace! The author? He lived out here, too?'' I questioned.

"Oh, for many years. He wrote several chapters of *Ben Hur* while staying with Old Mrs. Green. This was his writing desk and no doubt, it is priceless.'' Nellie was sitting near an old table that was so battered and beat up it didn't look like it was worth two bits.

"Thomas Edison. General Grant. Sarah Bernhardt. Governor Price. Lew Wallace. *Ben Hur*. Uhm,'' I mused, "if only these old walls could talk.''

Figuring on heads and counting beds, I had six more bedrooms. If anybody else came they could just sleep on the floor, or in the chicken coop for all I cared.

Mid afternoon on Friday, the house guests began arriving; Doris and Brian White and their three kids, Chris and Shirley Mansel, their two daughters and their two friends, Jack and Beth from New York.

Knowing the size of Rock House, Beth hadn't felt it necessary to inform us that Jack's eighteen-year old nephew, Paul would be with them.

Paul was a strapping hulk of an overgrown, typically New York teenager. His ego matched his size. On his way out, he had assured his aunt and uncle that he planned to spend the entire summer at the ranch and before he left he intended to be the best cow puncher that ever hit the southwest.

Nineteen of us could not squeeze around the dining room table so the five younger kids ate at a card table. I had dreaded being 'chief cook and bottle washer' for this mob but the Mansels had brought enough food for an army and so had the Whites. I had more help than I knew what to do with, so in far less time than I'd expected our first dinner was prepared, cooked, eaten with gusto and the last clean dish was stacked in the cupboard.

Shirley lit her favorite antique lamps, turned out the electric lights and clapped her hands for silence. "Nellie, our new visitors have not heard the history of this old house. How about some of your favorite stories?'' She asked.

Nellie was a fabulous story teller. If she couldn't find a good subject, she'd make one up. She had been Poet Laureate of Texas when she was in college and her gift of both writing and speaking had increased with age and wisdom.

"Anything in particular, Shirley? Which one do you think they'd enjoy most?" She asked.

"Gottschalk!" Chris bellowed before Shirley could answer. "What's better than that old goat?"

"But he's not a goat." Glenda protested. She had crawled up on Henry's lap. "He's our friendly ghost. We used to take food upstairs to him till Mommie made us stop. She said it got rotten and smelled bad."

When the laughter subsided, Nellie began: "This happened before the turn of the century, along about 1890 and not too long before Old Mrs. Green sold the Palace Hotel. Mr. Green was dead, the kids gone and after having been so busy all her life, Mrs. Green was very much alone and lonesome. Mr. Gottschalk was one of her last boarders. He was a bachelor, a scientist, often moody, tempermental and always forgetful. He lived on the third floor, in the two north rooms.

"One evening he burst into Mrs. Green's room, hollering 'This house is on fire!' Yes, the smell of smoke was very strong. She followed him to the other wing of the house and down the hall. 'You go that way, Mr. Gottschalk, I'll check this way.' As he disappeared so did the smell of smoke. When they returned to the hall, the smell of burning cloth was even stronger. After frantic searching they finally located the fire. It was in Mr. Gottschalk's pocket where he had stuck a still lighted pipe. A large hole was smoldering in his jacket pocket.

"Mr. Gottschalk was also erratic. If he missed a meal it was because he was engrossed in a scientific problem and prefered to be left undisturbed. So Mrs. Green wasn't upset when he missed three meals in one day but on the following morning she found his stone-stiff body hanging from the transom where had had hanged himself. This was the final straw. Mrs. Green was distraught and completely alone. Thus, when a few days later, all her chickens were stolen she finally decided to sell the house. She packed her small suitcase with her few possessions and walked away.

"So many strange, unaccountable things had happened since we bought this old Hotel that Henry and I, we were alone here at the time, decided to see if we could get any information on a rumored ghost from anyone around here.

"Our attempts at getting answers from the Cerrillos residents were frustrating; silence, nervous laughter, suspicious stares. But the strange happenings continued: doors opening and closing without reason, banging loudly in awesome stillness, floors creaking abnormally and even occasional discernable footsteps. All in all, more frustrating than frightening.

"Margaret Day, you were a victim of Gottschalk's antics soon after your arrival. Tell us about the 2 × 4 studs in his bedroom." Nellie requested.

"Ok, if you insist, Mother." I said. "At the tail end of a three day fall roundup, Henry got caught in the first blizzard of the year while loading his cattle to take to auction. He expected to be gone only overnight and finally got home four days later. I was in the house alone oiling our bedroom floors. As I went diligently about my task, a subtle, indeed strange change in the room's atmosphere began to make itself unmistakably felt. Stealthily, the patches of brilliant sunshine paled on my newly oiled floor and an eerie chill permeated the room. A feeling of aloneness overwhelmed me, yet I felt surrounded by a ghostly, uncanny presence. I'd heard vague rumors of the Palace Hotel being haunted, rumors which I received with a hearty pooh-pooh. But in this engulfing gloom, the increasing cold, this deathly quiet, I became apprehensive, even alarmed. There was a paradox in feeling completely alone and strange, yet in the company of an unknown, unearthly presence.

"Suddenly there was a tremedous crash on the third floor. With a shriek, I jumped halfway to the ceiling and raced out of the house as if pursued by the devil himself. I stood in the middle of the street, shiviering as the snowflakes gained momentum, and glared back at the house as if it had done me physical harm." I took a sip of coffee and chuckled.

"My mind started the craziest dialogue. Reason demanded a sensible approach; return and investigate that crash. My fear held me frozen in my tracks. Reason finally prevailed and reluctantly I forced myself to go up to the third floor. My fear increased with every step, I've never been so terrified, before or since.

"Henry and I had stacked four 2 × 4s behind a door and he had wired the door securely to the wall. One of those 2 × 4s was smack dab in the middle of the room."

There was a long pause. Grinning behind his mustache, Henry said: "Damndest thing I ever saw. Still can't figger it out!"

After a short, instrospective silence and before Nellie had a chance to continue, Chris asked Nellie to tell the tale about Old John, the tailor. "That's my favorite story, Nellie. I've been waiting for it."

The coffee pot and the bourbon bottle made another round. Nellie started, "Old John was an itinerant tailor. He was Hungarian by birth and had a delightful accent. For thirty years he had traveled this part of the country with his fashion sketches, material swatches, tape measure and order blanks. He had been a frequent guest at the Palace Hotel before Dr. Henry and I bought it. Old John stopped by one afternoon shortly after Henry and I moved in and I was about to turn him away. Henry came to the door and told me that John had been staying here for years and we should find a room for him.

" 'Thank you Henry, Mrs. Trigg.' He said as he bowed from the waist. 'I sleep in my car before I spend a night in that hotel in Madrid.' John returned several times, always to spend a night or two and even made some clothes for Henry.

"Well, the last time he came was the latter part of November and it was bitter cold. We had finished most of the remodeling, Margaret Day and the children weren't here, so Henry and I had moved downstairs to conserve heat. When bedtime came, I told Old John to sleep in the 'Death Room'..."

" 'Death Room!' " Beth interrupted. "Why was a room *ever* named that?"

Nellie deviated from her story to explain: "Years ago, Dr. Palmer had his office and operating room upstairs in the two adjoining rooms. The most convenient room for convalescing patients was directly across the hall. Medical and sanitary conditions being what they were at that time..." Nellie shrugged. She did not need to elaborate.

"Ugh!" Beth declared. "I hope we're not sleeping there! That could be one of Gottschalk's favorite rooms!"

Amid mixed voices of amazment and amusement, Chris answered: "Don't worry, Beth. That's our room. Go on with your story, Nellie."

"Well, John didn't know it as the 'death room' but I did tell him that we had installed a new bathroom in the room next to his and that it was heated and that he would not have to come downstairs to use the privy. I distinctly remember his appreciation.

"I was sleeping in the room right below his and was almost

asleep when thud, one of John's shoes hit the floor. I stayed awake, waiting for the second thud. It never hit. I was almost asleep again when I was startled to consciousness by slow, heavy steps coming down the stairs. I thought to myself, why is that crazy old man coming downstairs since I had explained to him about the bathroom upstairs? I waited and waited but not another sound. I finally fell into a deep sleep and didn't wake up till dawn the next morning.

"About eight o'clock he came in for breakfast. He was on his second cup of coffee as I was putting his eggs and bacon in front of him and I asked: 'John, why did you come downstairs last night?' 'But Mrs. Trigg, I did not come downstairs last night. I went right to bed.' He looked very perplexed and did not touch his breakfast.

"Well, I was somewhat perplexed myself and so I asked him: 'did you hear footsteps coming downstairs after you went to bed?' 'Yes, I heard steps but there are usually so many people in the house I never gave it a thought.' Then half under his breath, he added, 'This has happened to me before.' He still did not eat.

"I turned to Henry and asked if he'd heard steps. 'Sure I heard them but I thought it was you, John.' He looked at John as if to confirm his statement. John's only reaction was a strange look and again a muffled 'This has happened to me before.' He had not touched his breakfast.

"Then Henry said, 'Aw, it's nothing, Mother. Someone must have come in from the miners quarters and we didn't hear them go upstairs but we did hear them come downstairs.'

Nellie paused in her story and looked around at the expectant faces. "I must explain to you that we had rented the old dining room and two bedrooms right above it to a mining company from Moline, Missouri. They were prospecting for gold on Henry's ranch." She continued. "I was getting as agitated as Old John and said to Henry 'I guess I forgot to tell you, Henry, but the company foreman said it was too cold to work and they would return in the spring. I have nailed up the door and caulked it to keep out the cold drafts.'

'Mother, you are kidding me, aren't you?' Henry asked, leaving little doubt that he was hoping I was.

'No.' I answered. 'I am not kidding. Let's just go to that door and you can see for yourself.'

"Old John had still not touched his breakfast. He followed us. The door was exactly as I'd told them, nailed and caulked. I was real proud of my caulking job, the first time I'd ever had a caulking gun in my hands.

'This has happened to me before!' Old John wailed. He flew upstairs hastily packed his few belongings and was at the front door with hat in hand. Bowing from the waist he said to me, 'Mrs. Trigg, I hope you'll be...' he could not finish the 'all right.' He stammered again. 'I pray nothing will...' Again he could not finish. He looked wildly around and declared in a loud voice 'This has happened to me before!' He ran to his car and sped away.

"As Henry and I were returning to the kitchen, he said rather sadly, 'This is the last we'll ever see of Old John.' I contradicted him. 'Of course he'll be back. He hates that hotel in Madrid and said he'd *never* stay there.'

'Don't kid yourself, Mother. This *has* happened to him before. If you knew all the facts and figures about the old Palace Hotel, you'd realize that this was the day Old Mrs. Green found Gottschalk hanging from the transom.'

There was a very long pause. Then Jack asked, "Nellie, did Old John ever come back?"

"Yes." Nellie answered sadly. "About six months later. He stopped by to see if I was all right. He had stayed at the hotel in Madrid."

Nellie rose from the table with the dignity of a great lecturer leaving his lectern amid cries of "Please Nellie!" "Just one more story!"

"Not tonight." she smiled. "It's past midnight and by the time everyone gets to bed it will be even later. I'll tell you more tomorrow night."

No one had paid the slightest attention to Paul. He was sitting in a far corner, his eyes as big as Old John's cup of untouched coffee. I shuddered and thought to myself, Dear Lord! Where is he going to sleep? I had not expected him and worse, I'd forgotten all about him. Then I remembered the room on the third floor across the hall from Gottschalk's bedroom.

"Paul, you won't have to sleep on the floor after all. I do have one bed left over but you'll have to wait a little while till I get everyone else settled. OK?"

He had no alternative. He waited.

Among the list of renegades, wanted outlaws, would be wranglers and cowpokes that had crossed the threshold of Rock House, none was more unique than Henry's present cow hand. His name was Cooper Gillespie and he claimed to be a nephew of Billy the Kid. Strangely, he had asked Henry if he could have Gottschalk's room. He liked the old Victorian bed with the waist-high footboard and shoulder-high headboard. His working habits were erratic; if he came down for breakfast, he was on the job. If not, we might not see him for days or until he sobered up. He was the original 'hippie.' Twice a year he got a haircut, whether he needed one or not. Between these times his hair resembled a lion's mane, color and all, and would hardly have fit under a bushel basket, let alone the Stetson hat he somehow managed to cram it under. Drunk or sober, he always took off his boots and silently crept up the two flights of stairs, so we never knew when he was in the house.

Eventually I got the guests pigeonholed and returned for Paul. He seemed glued to the corner, his eyes still as big as saucers.

"Come on, Paul. I've got the rest of them bedded down and I can take you to your room now. Follow me." I said.

We crossed the yard, then climbed the long, dimly lighted stairs up to the second floor. "Where are Uncle Jack and Aunt Beth sleeping?" Paul asked.

I pointed. "Down this hall, then to the left and their room is at the end of the other hallway."

The ceiling light in the entrance hall was still on so we were not in total darkness. Each floor had a light at the top of the stairs with the usual pull chain. My problem was to find that chain at the top of the third floor stairs. The light was sufficient for us to see the steps to the third floor so I did not pull on the second floor light. However, before starting up, I checked my pocket. Yes, I had three kitchen matches but no sense in wasting them. I'd wait till we got to the top of the stairs. Then I struck one on my thumb nail. In the blackness, the sudden illumination was like a flash of lightning.

At least it must have seemed like lightning to Cooper Gillespie. He was asleep, stark naked, though hidden behind the footboard, in Gottschalk's room directly in front of us with the door wide open. He rose out of bed like a flesh and blood ghost, saw us in the flickering match light and grabbed for covers letting out a yowl. The vision of that wild lion's mane looming above the footboard was startling to me, terrifying to Paul!

Paul let out several screams you could have heard in Santa Fe, wheeled and in a bound was at the bottom of the stairs, tearing down the halls to his aunt and uncle's room. No one was asleep yet.

Doors popped open and people poured out, following those piercing sounds. Paul did not pause to knock on the door, it's a wonder he didn't just knock it down, nor did he halt once inside the safety of the room. He let out a final screech and with a huge leap, landed in bed between them. It was too much for the old-time slats. The bed collapsed. All three of them landed on the floor, the tall head and footboards careening threatingly above them. Within moments, the room was full of curious, frightened, concerned or amused observers.

"What's happened?" "What in heavens name..." "What's going on around here?" were the shouts heard above Paul's wails. Over that din, trying to be heard was almost impossible. I started to explain and the moment I mentioned Cooper's name, just the vision brought peals of laughter. The harder I tried to be heard, the louder the laughter.

Beth and Jack were trying vainly to disentangle Paul from their midst and Paul was making it quite obvious that he had no intention of being removed. He fully expected to be sheltered between them the rest of the night.

Jack rolled off the mattress, grabbed Pete's wrists and started tugging. Beth braced herself against the wall, placing both her feet in the middle of Paul's backside and gave a mighty shove. Jack's feet slipped and Paul sprawled spread eagle across his uncle's belly, a loud groan accompaning the breath that had been squashed out of him. Our laughter gave way to mild hysteria. Paul rolled over on all fours and started crawling back toward the bed. Beth was on her haunches like a fierce lioness fending off an attack.

"Oh no you don't!" She screamed to be heard over the noise. "You are *not* getting back in this bed tonight!"

"But Aunt Beth!" He pleaded. "You're not going to send me back upstairs to that ghost. You can't! *Please* don't send me back upstairs!"

Beth was guarding a frontal attack, Jack poised at the rear, ready to pounce on Paul's feet if he made the slightest move toward the bed. He remained motionless, his pitch black eyes searching in useless pleading.

At the top of her lungs, Beth yelled, "Maggie, what in the world happened? Everybody seems to know but us! How 'bout letting us in on all the fun?"

"I've been trying to tell you but I can't get this motley crew to pipe down. Now quiet. QUIET! All of you!" I had to yell.

Hysteria wound down to giggles.

"Who *is* Cooper?" Jack growled.

Threatening physical harm to anyone with more than a grin, I replied, "Cooper is Henry's cowpoke." I then related the incident.

"But what is that thing on his head?" Paul implored. "Does he sleep with that on every night?"

"That's just his hair, Paul. His natural hair. He's allergic to haircuts." I answered. I could no longer control the laughter. Finally I could add, "Come on, Paul. Cooper's the best protection you could have. Why, he even sleeps in Gottschalk's room."

Paul looked longingly at the bed, at Jack, at Beth. He knew there was no way he could get back into that bed and staying any longer would be very damaging to his ego. It was already badly dented. He followed me meekly but waited at the foot of the stairs till the light was on in his room. I realized he was empty-handed.

"Your suitcase, your pajamas, where are they?"

"Never mind. I won't need 'em tonight. I'll just sleep in my clothes." He answered.

I shrugged. "Want me to turn off the light before I go down?"

"NO!" He shouted. "Oh, pardon me. I mean 'no thank you.' I'll turn it off later."

According to Cooper the next morning, the light never got turned off. "I peeped in on him several times. He was sittin' bolt upright, clutchin' a pocket knife. Don't think he even closed his eyes and don't think he saw nothin' either, 'cause his eyes was kinda glazed. Say, what was all that hullabaloo last night. Never heard such a cacklin' and never thought it'd quit. Kept me wake half the night."

Through giggles and laughter, I finally explained. "Well I'll be! I'll just be damned." There was a long pause. "Where's this Paul right now? I think I ought to meet him proper."

I looked to Beth to answer. "Sorry, Cooper. I think you are too late to be properly introduced. He and his Uncle Jack are on the way to Santa Fe. The first bus back to New York leaves at 7:30."

CHAPTER 10
WIRELESS COMMUNICATION

Glenda had taken to nearly all aspects of ranch life like a duck to water, especially to horses. She loved them; big ones, small ones, gentle ones and wild ones, and they all loved her in return. After one of Henry's typical "Can't never could do anything" replies to her plaintive requests, "Henry would you help me up on my horse, I can't reach him" she had learned to do it herself. She had learned to bridle and saddle all but the wild broomies but she was much too little to mount by herself. She was forced to figure out how to maneuver her horse next to the large watering trough or to a sturdy wood fence. By the time she was eight, Glenda was one of the best 'cowpokes' Henry had. What she lacked in size, ability or expericence she made up for in trying and trust, which was far more than Henry could say for many a cowhand.

One morning Nellie and I were bantering back and forth over what wallpaper to use for the next project, Henry and Glenda were talking quietly but intently at the other end of the table. On a ranch every activity, even the fun ones such as riding (for a young kid) must have some practical purpose. She was getting instructions as to where to ride and what to look for. I paid little attention to those conversations. They often teased me by saying "Maggie can't find her way out of a paper bag." It was largely true. I would have been lost before I got out of sight of the corral.

Glenda had packed a small lunch, stuffed it in her jacket pocket, filled her canteen and jammed an old hand-me-down Stetson hat on her towhead and kissed me good-by. No one paid much attention to what horse she saddled unless Henry was going to ride, then he told her what horse *not* to ride.

I was too preoccupied that morning with gathering my tools for the day to notice that it had taken much longer than usual to coax her horse up to the trough. He was a green bronc that she'd been breaking and he had had a saddle on his back only a half dozen times. The first time, after the horse had smelled the saddle and became familiar with it, she set the saddle on the edge of the trough, maneuvered the horse close enough, then climbed on the trough and eased the saddle on his back, talking to him all the while. He didn't like it but he didn't offer too much resistance as she was holding him closely by the hackamore, patting him on the shoulder and quietly reassuring him. Then she led him around the corral till he

87

was 'walking easy.'

Several mornings later, after the saddle was firmly in place, she tightened the cinch and he pitched and "crow-hopped" until she calmed him down. The next morning when she tightened the cinch, he only snorted. She felt he was ready for the final test.

She led him around the lot, back and forth several times close to the trough, all the while explaining what she was going to do. She stopped him close to the trough and before he realized it, she was upon his back. This he did not like at all! He pitched, bucked, and snorted. She pulled the reins tight, held him in and spoke more firmly. After a few incensed cries, circles and stiff-legged hops around the lot he settled down, skittered, snorted some more, then stood, trembling slightly, shaking his head. She trotted him around the lot. What nice gaits he had. It was the beginning of a beautiful relationship. That little tyke was in love with that beautiful wild young horse, and apparently, he with her.

This particular morning Glenda was going to ride him out of the corral for the first time, on a long ride way up beyond the Old Dolores Mine to accomplish Henry's errand. Eventually she had him saddled, mounted and was on her way. As I watched her ride off on that sleek, beautiful young horse I felt more than ever like a two-legged pack mule as I lugged my supplies up those nineteen steps to begin my day's project.

The lack of any building codes in those days, the many years of settling and ravaging results of the elements and there was not a straight wall, window, door or ceiling in the entire house. Starting in the middle of a wall with a plumb line and sticking strictly to its guide was the only hope of having the wall paper going in some semblance of vertical order. It was lunch time before I got my paper measured and cut and about two in the afternoon before I got the nail holes plastered, the walls sized and the plumb lines marked. I was half way up the tall stepladder, unfolding my third strip of pasted paper when a wee small voice inside my head called:

"Go find your child!"

I was astounded and perplexed. I wasn't accustomed to hearing wee small voices. My 'reason' took over.

'I've got to finish this strip. I hardly have a foot leftover and I can't afford to waste it.'

"Get off that ladder and go find your child!" The voice was more insistent.

Now I was concerned. 'but I don't have the slightest idea where she is,' reason contended.

"Go find your child!"

I flipped the paper paste-side up over the top of the ladder, hoping it would dry okay and I could use it later, quickly rinsed the sticky paste off my hands and dried them on my shirt tail as I flew out the door. Thank goodness, Henry had not taken my car today. As I was running out, Nellie called, "Where are you going, Margaret Day?"

"Oh, just a small errand. Be back in a little while." The voice had been strongly persistent and urgent, but I did not want to worry Mother.

As I started the car I thought, where in Heaven's name should I go to find her in 30,000 acres? Why hadn't I been more attentive to Henry's morning instructions? Even if I had been, I probably wouldn't have known where to look. Should I cross the railroad tracks and go over Devil's Throne? Should I cross the bridge and head toward Madrid? Or go up the east side of the Ortiz Mountain? These questions were crowding through my mind as I slowly drove the two blocks to the intersection. Without being conscious of it, I turned the car right, down the main street and across the bridge. I did not think. Nor do I remember hearing that voice again. And I wasn't consciously aware that I had inwardly asked for help in these decisions. The car took the first left fork and soon I shifted down to low gear as it started up the rough, rocky, washed-out road toward the Old Dolores Mine.

I was not overly worried and I did not seem to be driving the car. I was merely behind the steering wheel, turning it to avoid the deepest ruts and the largest stones and to keep it on the road, such as it was. Then as I rounded a huge clump of cedar brush I saw Glenda. Apprehension *and* relief short-circuited my brain. I sat behind the wheel, dazed.

I had not realized that she had ridden the bronc! Tied securely to the saddle horn was her rope. On the end of that rope was a yearling colt that Henry had been searching for. Henry was afraid that it might have been stolen, or worse yet, might be running with the wild bunch. Glenda, the bronc and the colt were having a tug of war behind a barbed wire gate which she couldn't get close enough to open.

When I had sufficiently recovered my senses and my voice, I

quietly got out of the car and walked to the wire gate that separated us and in a tone that I hoped did not show my true emotions I asked, "Glenda, can I give you a hand?" Dumb question!!

"Yes, Mommie. Would you please open the gate?" Was her unperturbed answer. "But first you'd better hide the car behind those trees. Neither of these colts is used to cars and I won't be able to get them through the gate if it's in sight."

I was thankful for the opportunity to collect myself. She was patiently waiting until I returned to the gate and the horses had settled down. It was only the 'quiet before the storm!' As they started through the opening, both horses bolted, in opposite directions. A powerful struggle was in progress, again with tiny little Glenda in the middle. I was amazed at the ability, the courage and the physical strength it took to get through that gate. When she finally had her animals under control and I could talk to her, my questions came tumbling out.

"Glenda, what are you doing with that colt? Did Henry ask you to bring him in today? How on earth did you manage to rope him?"

"This is the colt that Henry thought was running with the broomies." She replied matter-of-factly. "He asked me to keep a look out for him. When I found him I thought I'd try to bring him in. He was a little hard to catch in these cedars, but I finally got a rope on him."

"Then what happened?"

"Nothing. Well, not exactly nothing. I couldn't get my horse close enough to the gate to open it. Every time I could almost reach it, either my horse shied away or the colt pulled him away. I didn't dare get off to open it because there wasn't any way I could get back on again and if these two horses had gotten away from me they would have ruined the saddle and killed each other, being tied together. Then Henry would have killed me."

Again her calm word struck terror in my heart. "How long have you been here?" If I kept on talking maybe that awful feeling would go away.

"Oh, I don't know. I can't tell you excatly. Maybe thirty minutes, maybe more." She answered.

Then the question I dreaded, "If I had not come along, what would you have done?"

"I knew somebody would come."

"Weren't you even worried, Glenda?"

A perplexed expression crossed her face. "No, Mommie. Why should I have been worried?" She didn't give me time to answer and quickly continued, "When I knew I wasn't going to be able to do it myself, I just said, Please dear God, it doesn't look like I can do it by myself so please send someone to help me." There was a long pause. "I wasn't worried. I knew He would send you or Henry or Fritz or somebody to help me."

We looked deep into each others eyes, not the look between a mother and her child but between two people, two individuals with no time, no years separating their understanding and trust and faith. Words were not necessary.

Finally. "I'll close the gate, Glenda. Do you want me to wait and follow you down?"

"No, Mommie. I'm all right now. I know you're busy with your wallpapering so go on home. I'll be there pretty soon."

I returned to the wallpapering as if nothing too extraordinary had happened, on the outside, that is. Inside my soul, however, there was a warm glow that will never burn itself out, the cementing of an ESP between Glenda and myself that is almost as strong some thirty-odd years later as it was that afternoon.

CHAPTER 11
HOLLYWOOD—CERRILLOS STYLE

Nellie's conception of driving a car was: the proper position of the accelerator was on the floor; 'a miss is as good as a mile;' let someone else wear *their* brakes out; if your horn didn't honk the car was caput. However, she was an excellent driver and it was only her passengers who suffered.

One morning, after a grueling bout with town and the 'cherrand list' and enveloped in her own cloud of dust, she skidded to a stop in front of Rock House. A strange hitching post that had not been there when she'd left a few hours earlier was right smack in front of the entrance. It did nothing to improve her already distraught disposition. She blasted the horn three long honks (her signal for us to come-a-running whenever, wherever we heard it), jumped out of the car and started yelling before Henry had time to move.

"God o' Mercy! Who put that hitching post there? Who gave anyone permission to put that thing in front of my house?"

Before she could shout any more questions, a man came running out of the front door, also yelling at the top of his voice. "Who put that big black car in front of my hitching post? Who owns that black thing? Tell 'em to get if out of...!"

Nellie, by now standing directly in front of the man, continued shouting. "I happen to own that 'black thing' and I also happen to own this house and just what is that hitching post doing in front of it? Get your hitching post off my property and *now!*"

"Your property! Your property!!" He yelled back. "I got permission from Mr. Trigg to put that hitching post up and I'm not taking it down until I'm good and ready to!"

Henry, not having an opportunity to explain to either of the arm-waving contenders, came running. "Wait! Wait a minute, you two. Calm down. It's all very simple. Mr....I forgot your name." Henry said.

"Jasper. Tony Jasper," was his curt answer.

"Mother, this is Tony Jasper. Mr. Jasper, my mother, Mrs. Trigg. She does own the house and the black car." Henry explained.

Before Henry could make any more explanations, Mr. Jasper in a most gracious manner, stuck his hand toward Nellie. "I'm so sorry, Mrs. Trigg." He said in a conciliatory voice. "Your son gave us permission to put up the hitching post. If you don't mind, we want to use this beautiful old place for a few scenes in a movie we're making. As soon as we're finished, we'll gladly take it down."

Nellie's graciousness instatnly matched his. "Oh, of course, Mr. Jasper, you can finish your filming. I just wasn't here when all this happaened and was taken by surprise."

"Mr. Jasper and his people arrived soon after you left, Mother, so we couldn't ask your permission." Henry explained. "They just wanted to make a few shots and I didn't think you'd mind. They'll be taking it down real soon."

"Mrs. Trigg, do you mind if we move your car. Our picture wouldn't be quite..."

Nellie interrupted. "Oh, certainly. I'll drive it around to the side and take things out..."

She was interrupted. "That won't be necessary, Mrs. Trigg." He whistled. Two handsome young men, dressed in full western frontier regalia, dogtrotted through the front door. "Your keys, please, Ma'am." The car was moved and unloaded like magic.

As Nellie was going into the kitchen she asked, "Have you and your crew had lunch? I rather doubt it as there isn't a place around here where you can eat. Let me fix something for you."

"Thank you very much, Mrs. Trigg, but we did bring box lunches." Mr. Jasper answered.

"A cup of coffee perhaps?" Nellie suggested.

"If it isn't too much trouble, we'd be delighted, Mrs. Trigg." Mr. Jasper answered.

"Not at all. Let me know when you are ready and how many cups to make." Nellie said.

When the filming was finished, Mr. Jasper, the crew with their box lunches, joined Nellie and Henry around the table for coffee. Unexpected plans for Rock House were in the making.

"Mrs. Trigg, I have been searching everywhere for a suitable location to make a western movie. This house, this ranch, this land, everything is more perfect than any set designer could ever dream, let alone construct. Would you and your son consider letting us use it as our location? You'd be paid, of course."

Mother and son exchanged looks, then nods of approval. "I see no reason why not." Nellie answered.

"And please, Mrs. Trigg," Mr. Jasper continued, "would it be possible for us to rent a few rooms in the house so the cast could stay here and not have to search for quarters elsewhere?"

"Oh, Mr. Jasper, much as I'd like to, that's impossible. I can't find anyone to help for just Henry and myself. And your entire cast? There are plenty of rooms, but the cooking, the housekeeping. I do hate..."

"Please, Mrs. Trigg." Mr. Jasper interrupted. "You won't need any outside help. You'll have more help than you'll know what to do with."

Again Nellie looked at Henry quizzically; he seemed quite comfortable with the idea. Nellie had always been a pushover for an entertaining guest and now she could have a house full of them! The deal was quickly struck. Rooms were assigned and preliminary instructions were issued. The coffeepot made another round, the director, his actors, Nellie and Henry toasted each other with hand shakes and smiles of satisfaction in anticipation of a new adventure.

As filming commenced, a loose routine developed. Breakfast and lunch were unplanned and haphazard. People ran to and fro, grabbing a bite or a cup of coffee as time permitted. Evenings, however, were another matter. The day's work over, all had an opportunity to relax, have a drink or whatever suited, then share the evening meal and stories. The dining table could not accomodate the entire cast at one sitting, so the extras ate first and the stars had the second sitting so they could remain around the table to be entertained by Nellie for as long as she was willing to keep them spellbound with her yarns and stories, fact or fiction — who cared!

One evening they ganged up on her. Nellie was the 'star' but did not know it. A microphone was concealed at the head of the table where she presided. A recorder was hidden in one side of the huge oak sideboard. On the pretense of wanting to know more about the area, various members asked her questions and in this way got her to tell them all about the history of the area, the stories about the turquoise mines and some of the legends connected with mining.

"An interesting story surrounds the mine now known as the Chalchihuitl, just a few miles from here. The San Marcos Indians were working this mine when Coronado arrived and established his fort in Galisteo. Soon after, there was a terrible cave-in and many Indians were trapped and lost their lives. For many generations the superstition existed that the mine was evil and the Indians' unwillingness to work it kept it unexploited. It was not until the 19th century that it was reopened by a group of Irishmen. But once again, Indian superstition proved more powerful than logic and science. This time, in the form of the rattlesnake. To the Indians, the rattlesnake is sacred and is to be harmed under no circumstances. Thus, in all those years that the mine was abandoned, the snakes thrived and multiplied and proved to be far more dangerous than cave-ins, floods or broken cables. The mine was once again abandoned.''

"Mrs. Trigg, is turquoise the only thing that was mined in these parts?'' asked a cast member.

"Oh, good heavens no. Within a circumference of about twenty-five miles, right in this area, is supposed to be the richest concentration of minerals on the North American continent: coal, gold, lead, zinc, copper, even semi-precious stones such as garnets as fine as rubies were found near Cerrillos. Emeralds, small but very valuable, were found on the Lopez de Mecita Grant. Just across the San Marcos Creek you'll see the ruins of a once flourishing zinc and lead smeltering plant that operated from 1902 until not too many years ago. It supplied electricity to some of the establishments here in Cerrillos who wanted it. All that remains are the stone foundations of the plant and aqueduct. Even the slag heap is disappearing under the shovel of souvenir seekers and the ravages of time and wind.

"Many of the historical records were destroyed with the Indian uprisings, first the Pueblo Indians in New Mexico in 1680, then the Pimas in Arizona in 1751.

"This much is fairly well authenticated, however. Gold mining was started in the early seventeenth century in the 'Mina del Tierra' mine near here but was also abandoned because of the Indian rebellion. In 1713 an account of a covered mine was recorded in the archives in Santa Fe, known as 'The Lost Spanish Mine,' it is located somewhere in the Ortiz Mountains. Henry keeps hoping it is on his land and he will be able to find it.''

"There's still 'gold in them thar hills'.'' Henry chuckled as he interrupted. "Just wish I could find it!''

Nellie continued, "The placer mines, 'La Bolsa' are on Henry's land and no one will ever know the amount of gold that was crudely dug out of those pock holes by pick and shovel. One of the largest gold nuggets in history was found on the ground up on the 'Dolores Grant.' That started the New Mexico 'gold rush' in 1826 that lasted until 1914 and before the turn of the century, over $3,000,000.00 worth of gold was taken from the Dolores Grant.

"And wasn't coal mined here too?'' asked another member of

the cast.

"Well, yes, and still is," Nellie continued, delighted by her audience's interest in one of her favorite subjects. "I've already told you that the Green family built this house and lived here many, many years. Mrs. Green's daughter told me this story. Every day her two older brothers took the goats up to the Ortiz Mountains to graze. On several occasions they noticed sparks flying from the goats' hooves as they jumped over a steep embankment. Full of curiousity, the boys pried loose some chunks of the black stones and took them home to their father. Coming from the coal mining region of Kentucky, Mr. Green immediately recognized it as rich rainbow coal. Soon after the first coal mines were opened and people flocked in by the hundreds. The original partnership Mr. Green formed ended in a dispute with his partner who set fire to the mine. It is still burning to this day but the supply of coal in this area was so plentiful that other shafts were sunk.

"Almost overnight this peaceful little village became the hub of trememdous activity. The stagecoach route had been enlarged and improved but not so the housing accomodations. It was then that Mr. Green's dream of a "Palace Hotel" became a reality. The addition was not to be built of adobe as was the first house which had been built by the Indians from adobe bricks. For years the old adobe building had been used as a trading post and the upper room served as a storehouse for the hides and pelts the trappers had brought from hundreds of miles around. Perhaps Kit Carson was among those hearty trappers who stored his pelts here? Later, that same room became the first Masonic Lodge in the New Mexico Territory and Mr. Green became a 32nd Degree Mason.

"The 'Palace Hotel' was indeed a palace. The best stonemasons of the day were hired and a regal colonial mansion was built, each handhewn stone laid with the precision of a brick. The arches above the tall windows were chiseled with as much care as if for cathedral windows. The furnishings were equally as magnificent: Brussels carpets, crystal candleholders, Spode china, velvet draperies over lace curtains, an elaborate water system with drainage to the San Marcos Creek and a central carbide heating system.

"When the lead and zinc mines were started, the Greens again enlarged their hotel. The rooms were occupied almost before they were finished. the unfortunate ones who Mrs. Green could not accomodate as roomers were not denied the privileges of her 'board' for which she was famous. She either cooked or supervised every meal that came from her enormous stove, and no record could ever verify the hundreds of meals she served."

"Mrs. Trigg, somehow I got lost in time. What dates are you telling about?"

"We're talking about the 1880's, long before the turn of the century." Nellie answered. "By this time, Cerrillos had become an incorporated town with its own water system, hard surfaced streets, a fire department and the Hurt Opera House was the largest one in the territory. In fact, in 1882, Sarah Bernhardt, or was it Lily Langtry? was called back for so many encores that she developed a sore throat and spent a week convalescing here with Mrs. Green — or so the story goes. Also, so it's been said, she and Mrs. Green became fast friends. In 1889 the finest school in the entire southwest was built on the west side of the Galisteo River. It, too, was built with handhewn, mason-laid native rocks, two-story, with eight of the finest equipped classrooms.

"But all was not industry, education or culture. One Sunday morning, shortly before breakfast, Mrs. Green sent one of her sons downtown, only a few blocks, for some necessary supplies to finish the morning meal. In a very short time, the lad returned popeyed and breathless but without completing his errand. He hadn't stopped to count the number of dead men in front of the many saloons — evidence of a rowdy night in town."

"Mrs. Trigg, the Greens must have been very important citizens here in Cerrillos. You mention them so often. What kind of people were they?"

"I'm glad you asked that question, Jake." Nellie answered. "Mrs. Green was a most unusual person. Everyone loved her. She was very talented and gifted and when it came to her children, she was clairvoyant. Clay, her oldest son, was unusually tall for those times, over six feet, two inches and extremely handsome. He had met Teddy Roosevelt and wanted to join his Rough Riders and be a part of the Spanish-American War. Mr. Roosevelt thought that Clay was too tall to be one of his regular soldiers but did commission him to be his Flag Bearer.

"One day, as Mrs. Green was preparing dinner for her many boarders, she threw her pan in the air and shrieked, "My Clay has just been killed. My Clay is dead! He was carrying his flag over the summit of San Juan Hill and they have shot and killed my Clay. I have just seen it all as if I had been standing there!" She was inconsolable.

"The days went by, but in due time she was summoned to the parlor. A grave young man, respectfully holding his hat in both hands, awaited her. 'Mrs. Green, I made a special trip here to see you. I was one of your son's best friends. I was standing almost next to Clay when he was...' Mrs. Green interrupted him. 'Yes, son, I know. You don't have to say it.'

'I know Clay would have wanted me to come to tell you.' He repeated word for word the incident as it has flashed through Mrs. Green's vision, at the exact moment it had happened. She thanked the young man but she did not tell him that she had seen the incident in a vision when it happened."

The room was silent. Nellie continued. "Then there was the younger brother, Calvin. He was killed in an explosion at the Stevens Mine in Las Cruces, New Mexico. At the instant that it occured, Mrs. Green pictured in her mind the horrifying details of that deadly explosion. There was no communication to let Mrs. Green know about the fatal accident yet by the time they bore his body home in a wagon, she had finished all the funeral arrangements. As they carefully laid his battered, broken body in a simple wooden coffin, another picture flashed through Mrs. Green's clairvoyant vision. They had not found all of Calvin's body. His left leg had been blown off and was trapped under a huge timber. 'We can not have the funeral yet. We must wait, dear family and friends. Calvin must be buried with his other leg,' she told the waiting mourners. She described in minute detail the exact location of her son's missing leg; down which tunnel, into which chamber, and under a certain log. 'Ride on horseback, fast. We can not wait too long' were her parting words. The next afternoon, the sad, quiet funeral procession bore the coffin up the winding path to the Cerrillos graveyard. In the plain wooden box lay Calvin's complete body."

Nellie took a long drink of water to let the silence fill the room again.

"Another interesting story Nancy Green told me was about Roy, and the Ortiz Mine Robbery. Large quantities of gold were being mined at this mine and regular shipments of gold amalgam were shipped to the Denver, Colorado mint via Los Cerrillos. Roy Green was employed by the mine and was responsible for the safety of those shipments. On one occasion, Roy was driving the wagon from the mine to the railroad in Cerrillos when he was held up by a masked bandit, who, with the aid of a very persuasive 38 Colt, forced Roy to throw down the bag of gold. This particular shipment amounted to approximately $50,000.00. Roy, fortunately, was sent on his way unharmed but minus his precious cargo. The bandit then dug a hole and buried his loot for safekeeping against his return when the news and excitment of the robbery had abated. However, the entire robbery was witnessed by a sixteen-year old boy of Cerrillos, Maurice Utt, who had been sitting on the side of the hill, silently observing the procedure. After the bandit hid the gold, Maurice calmly dug it up and returned the entire amount to the mine foreman who paid him the sum of $50.00 as a reward."

"Oh, Mrs. Trigg, you do tell such fascinating stories. You make us feel like we knew Cerrillos in its heyday." Said the singing star, Bill Dicks.

"Mother, I think they would enjoy your story about the old Mexican sheepherder and the turquoise cave. This is a true story." Henry emphasized.

"Yes, it's true and one of my favorite stories." Nellie began enthusiastically. "There is positvie archeological evidence of the San Marcos Indian Pueblo not too many miles from here that simply vanished overnight and it became known as the 'Lost Tribe.'

"Rattlesnakes again, Mrs. Trigg? They seem so closely intertwined with Indian and turquoise legends," someone asked.

"No. Not rattlesnakes. Something far more fearsome and deadly! Slavery!" Again Nellie paused, sipped some water, letting the last word sink in dramatically. "Coronado's stronghold was not too many miles up the Galisteo River, about twenty miles. He was said to have had his bull pen where he kept his captive Indians, on the flat just west of here, where the San Marcos Creek empties into the Galisteo River. The San Marcos Pueblo was a profitable hunting ground for Coronado's warriors looking for Indian slaves. The Pueblo was rapidly being depleted of its braves so one night, no doubt after long and secret planning and with as few necessities as possible, they silently vanished into the darkness, never to be heard of again. The only explanation of their continued existence is that they must have melded into one of the other Pueblo Indian tribes farther to the north or east in an area less accessible to Coronado's marauders. But no one has ever actually determined where their stealthy disappearance led them.

"A good many years after their disappearance, again the date unknown, a Mexican sheepherder was taking his large flock across the San Marcos Creek, only seven miles from here on the Calvin Ranch. All but a dozen or so of the last stragglers had crossed the dry creek bed when he heard the distant but distinct rumblings of an approaching flash flood. He hurried the last animals to high ground but as he was scrambling up the last few feet of steep bank his footing gave way and he fell into a deep hole. Fortunately, he was not hurt and as his eyes became adjusted to the sudden darkness, he realized he was in a large room, not a natural cave. His first concern was to study the opening and determine how he was going to get out, but all he could see was a blinding patch of blue sky. He reached in his pocket for the dependable, ever present wood match and struck it across the seat of his pants. He stood transfixed. The ceiling was made of heavy timbers, buried beneath tons of adobe. As he glanced around the room, the flicker of his match reflected on strange, shiny objects and his immediate problem of how to escape from this eerie room was deflected by his curiosity. His eyes became more adjusted and as he crept deeper into the darkness he lit a second match. He stood and gasped! The walls were festooned with magnificent silver and turquoise necklaces, belts, bracelets, and rings.

As his eyes became more used to the dimness of the cave he could see that every wall contained countless pieces of rare and exquisite treasures, the like of which few people on earth have ever seen. He could not believe his eyes.

"If his eyes were unbelieving, not so his ears. The awesome silence in the silent tomb was broken by the increasing roar of the angry flash flood, gaining momentum every second. If he didn't hurry and get out, the next explorer would find his lowly bones amid this splendid array.

"He found a way out and, hurriedly stuffing his pockets as full as possible, scrambled up the fallen timber and squeezed through the hole. He reached the safety of the top of the bank just as a four-foot wall of muddy water was lunging at his heels."

Nellie took a long pause. "Then what happened, Mrs. Trigg? That's not the end of the story?" asked a disappointed voice.

"No, not exactly! The old herder stood for a long, long time, taking exact sightings from this cedar tree to that hill or boulder or to goodness-knows-what, as he fully expected to return again. He feared the cave might be at least partially filled with water but he knew the treasures would remain. He did return, many, many times but his sightings must have been faulty. He could never find his treasure cave again."

There were many disappointed Oh's and No's around the table. "Was the treasure cave ever found again?" asked Tony Jasper.

"No."

"Was it ever looked for again?"

"Was it ever!" Henry exclaimed. "Even I have looked for it! Old Tom Perkins, who worked for Frank Calvin for many years, built a shack on the bank of the San Marcos near the site of the 'Lost Tribe,' and got himself a plow and team of mules. Every minute he wasn't in a saddle he was behind the plow looking for the treasure. He never even found a splinter from the ceiling timbers!

"Did you ever find anything of interest, Henry?"

"Yeah. If I ever had a few extra hours, I'd go over and dig. I found a real good skeleton and lots of pieces of human bones and skulls, pockets full of arrows and bits of broken pottery, too." Henry answered.

"Do you have any of them? Could you show them to us?" It was a question full of anticipation.

"Fraid not. Kinda wish I had 'em but I took 'em all to the museum. You can see them there and some of the pieces of turquoise the old Mexican herder found, too. When he couldn't find his treasure room again, and not knowing what to do with the treasures, he took them all to the museum. They had never seen anything like these pieces and it was presumed that they were cermonial pieces from the 'Lost Tribe'!"

There were request for more stories but Nellie begged off saying, "It's almost midnight and this old lady is exhausted."

Then she noticed their smiles and surreptitious glances, "Say what have you been up to anyway?"

They roared with laughter while showing her the hidden mike and the recorder. Nellie was astounded but flattered and delighted. What I wouldn't give for that tape!!

CHAPTER 12
OSCAR AND THE CHICKENS

One naturally expects to find chickens running loose in the yard of a normal country home but ours was not normal. We had no chickens, that is not until someone wished a young rooster off on Henry soon after our arrival. I'm quite sure that whoever gave him to my bachelor brother had small children and wanted to protect their very lives or they had a severe grudge against Henry.

Oscar was a magnificent rooster, the most beautiful one I ever saw. He was also the meanest, most ornery creature to ever stalk the earth! The devil himself must have created Oscar in his own likeness. His feathers were fiery red, blending into tones of orange, bronze and brown. His brilliant red cock's comb stood straight and tall, almost two inches high and even his long spurs were tinged in red and rapier sharp. No one had the courage or fortitude to catch him and remove them.

Oscar was as arrogant as he was elegant, as fearless as he was mean and without one ounce of goodness or reason. He must have been the outcast from a long line of illustrious fighting cocks. Now he had no cocks to fight so he fought everbody and everything else. No doubt, he was snatched away from his harem in the dead of night and his prickly disposition was intensified by his frustration.

One of the unwritten ranch rules was "don't leave tools near traffic paths." However, with Oscar loose in the back yard, it was essential to carry some sort of tool for defense. The shovels, rakes and hoes came out in great array. Oscar knew those loathsome handles. If you have one in your hand, he would saunter close but not attack. But woe-be-unto-you if he found you empty-handed!

Pot also wasn't safe from attack. With scorn and dignity, Pot usually managed to stay out of Oscar's path but one afternoon Pot got careless and was attacked. He bit Oscar, not very hard, oh how easily he could have killed him, but a definite warning. Oscar was mean, not stupid; he left Pot alone after that.

We'd had that crazy rooster for about three weeks when I had an inspiration. "Where can we get some chickens, Henry? Maybe it would improve that old devil's disposition. And I could sure use some fresh eggs."

"Something's got to improve it or we're going to have rooster and dumplings!" Henry responded. "Yesterday I forgot my handle and that old devil knew I didn't have it. He was sneaking up behind me for an attack, I just happen to have looked over my shoulder in the nick of time and kicked backwards. I caught him under the chin and sent him flying. It shore made him mad!'' Henry chuckled. "Yep! Maybe some chickens would help. If not, he goes in the pot. I'll talk around, Maggie.''

Later that afternoon, Henry went visiting to his friend, Charlie Domineque, who seemed to know everything that went on in that area.

"Henry. I hear your neighbor gonna leave her husband and she gonna move to Santa Fe. Ma'be she wannna sell her chickens. You wan' me find out?'' Charlie asked.

"Sure, Charlie. That'd be great. Let me know as soon as you can, OK?''

Henry had put in his request just in the nick of time. Charlie stopped by the next evening. "Henry, you got yourself forty eight hens, young and healthy but you gotta get them. She let you know when you go get 'em.'' Charlie announced.

One evening a few days after Charlie had stopped by, I had cooked a large pot of spaghetti and made a big bowl of cole slaw, surely enough for more than supper, I thought. The lamps had already been lit, dinner was on the table and there was a knock on the door. Jimmy had bicycled down to tell us that the neighbor had phoned that tonight was convenient for us to come get her chickens.

In our excitment about the chickens, our scramble to gather enough sacks to bring them home in and our hasty departure I completely forgot to feed poor hungry Pot. As for us, we'd be ravenous on our return so I didn't bother to put the food away. I would just reheat the spaghetti when we got back.

I had experienced grabbing chickens off their roost in a dark hen house and stuffing them, squawking and flapping into a sack on the ranch in Texas but the kids had never had such fun. It was better than a circus. Between each raid, waiting for the hens to settle down, the kids would become very impatient. We finally bagged the last hen and I wrote a check for $48.00.

We returned home tired and hungry but excited. Our bubble burst when we saw the dining room table. It looked like it had been set for breakfast; not one morsel of food! Pot had never gotten on the table before. He even knew not to beg while we were eating. Perhaps he'd figured that if he could sleep on Henry's pillow why shouldn't he eat off Henry's table, especially since no one remembered to feed him. His hunger had gotten the best of him. He had devoured everything edible but miraculously maneuvered around those lighted kerosene lamps. Beads of cold sweat popped out when I realized what could have happened if those lighted lamps had been knocked over.

Henry was furious! He sat down on a chair against the wall and in his sternest voice said, "Pot, come here."

Pot hesitated. He didn't know what he'd done to deserve that tone in his master's voice. Several times Henry looked from Pot to the table. Pot followed his eyes.

"Pot Licker!" Henry commanded. "I said come here and sit!"

Pot still didn't move. He looked at Henry, the table, then the door. Several weeks before, Henry had replaced the spring on the screen door. It was as tight as a steel drum. Twice Pot had miscalculated its strength and it had slammed shut on his tail. Now he wouldn't go out that door unless someone held it open.

"Pot Licker! What have you done?" Henry demanded.

That removed all doubt from Pot's mind. He tucked his long tail between his legs, bolted for the door and was off into the night well before it banged shut. The kids had stifled their giggles when they realized the seriousness of Pot's offense but now they could no longer contain themselves. Neither could I. We had fits of laughter. Henry's face finally relaxed into a grin. "Dumb dog! I'll bet he doesn't do that again!"

"Dumb dog, my foot." I said. "That's the smartest dog I ever saw! Just what would you have done?"

Pot was not home the next morning, the next day or the day after. I was worried sick. All of us loved and depended on that dog more than we were willing to admit. Finally, on the fourth morning I could stand it no longer.

"Henry, where on earth do you suppose Pot could be? Do you think someone has stolen him, or killed him? Shouldn't we go look for him?" I was almost in tears.

"No, Maggie; he's just run away for a few days. He'll be all right and come wagging home when he gets hungry enough. Don't worry about him." Henry answered.

Later that morning, we drove to Henry's dug-out camp in the Jeep. On the way home, there sat Pot, sitting on his haunches, about fifteen feet off the road. He had heard the jeep drive by and was awaiting our return but was not sure of his reception. Henry stopped the Jeep and called, "OK Pot. All's forgiven. You can come home now."

Pot jumped in the Jeep and licked Henry's neck and head all the way home. The subject of the supper table was never mentioned. It wasn't necessary.

Because of Pot's hasty exit and long absence, he was not aware that the back yard would be full of new arrivals. He joyfully took after the closest one.

"Pot Licker!" Henry's sharp command stopped him dead in his tracks. "Don't you ever let me catch you chasing another chicken. They are Maggie's, and not your playmates." After that, Pot never bothered the chickens.

Oh what joy to have eggs, fresh eggs, all we could eat and some to share. But sad to say, it did not improve Oscar's disposition. It made him worse, more arrogant and cocky than ever! He had missed his harem and lost no time in asserting his male duties. But the children were alarmed at Oscar's savage attacks on the hens. One afternoon, Fritz had failed to arm himself against Oscar, and narrowly escaped to the safety of the gate. To flaunt his daring and relieve his frustration, Oscar spotted a little hen, peacefully scratching in the dust and according to Fritz, "He attacked her and she cackled so loud I thought he was killing her. So I decided to get even with the old devil."

He grabbed a nearby rake to defend himself and gathered a handful of rocks. Though he'd been practicing rock throwing he still wasn't too good a shot and it took three fair sized rocks before one connected smack on Oscar's head. It knocked him out cold. He lay motionless on the ground, not a feather stirring. Fritz bent down and watched intensely. No sign of life.

I just happened to be coming out of the kitchen and saw the lad stooping over the prostrate rooster. I called out, "Fritz, what's the matter with Oscar? He looks like he's dead."

"I think he is, Mother." He answered sadly.

By the time we met in the middle of the yard, big tears were trickling down his dust-covered face. "I think I killed him."

I gathered him close to me. He was a 'big boy' now and very seldom cried. "What happened, Frtiz?" I quietly asked.

By the time he'd finished his story, Oscar was beginning to come to. "See, he's going to be OK. You must have just stunned him." I said.

Nellie was delighted with our new addition of livestock. One afternoon she was making a packaged cake and needed two eggs. Glenda was engaged in her favorite pastime, dressing her reluctant cat in doll clothes. It was not easy to get her attention.

"Glenda, I think your cat has modeled enough for awhile. Run out to the hen house and get me two eggs, please." Nellie requested.

"But Nellie, I'm not through yet. Can't I do it later?" She protested.

"No. I'm making a cake and I need them..."

"Cake!" She yelled. She released her death grip on the squirming cat and flew out so fast she forgot the egg basket and her defense weapon. It seemed like hours and Glenda had still not returned.

"Margaret Day, go see what's happened to Glenda. Is she waiting for the hens to lay eggs?" Nellie asked.

I met Glenda at the door. Tears were trickling down her freckled cheeks and both stubby fists made lumps in her blue jeans pockets. "Pixie, what happened? Are you hurt?"

She shook her head and sniffled. "No, I'm not hurt. I'm all right."

"Where are the eggs?"

Very sheepishly, she unknotted her little fists and inched her hands out of her pockets, pulling them inside out, almost in slow motion, and showed us the slimy, gooey mixture of shell, yolk and white. Before either of us could say a word she blurted out. "It was that mean old Oscar! He was chasing me and I jumped up on the gate to get away from him and squashed the eggs." Then she really started crying. "And the reason it took me so long is 'cause I was looking for more eggs and they were the last two!"

Several months later, Nellie sent her fastest runner, Fritz, for breakfast eggs. He no longer bothered with a handle; he kept a pocket full of small stones. If Oscar even looked in his direction, a carefully placed stone would discourage another attack. In a very few minutes, Fritz ran in hollering, "Mother, Nellie, Henry! There aren't any chickens! They're all gone! Not one chicken! Not even old Oscar!"

"What are you saying, Fritz?" Nellie was the first to ask.

"Come'n see!" He insisted. "There is not one chicken in the yard, in the hen house or anywhere!"

We looked. He was right. There wasn't even one egg.

"Henry, do you suppose...?" Nellie asked.

He shrugged with a look of disgust. "Folks around here get hungry, too. Those fat hens make pretty good eating."

"Oh Henry!" I moaned. "You can't mean what you are saying! They wouldn't dare steal *all* of them, would they?"

"They're all gone, aren't they?" His tone clearly indicated that he thought that I was a very dumb sister.

Nellie sputtered "I think you should go right this minute and find out who stole them and get them all back!"

"Are you kidding, Mother! They're probably all in cooking pots by now!"

CHAPTER 13

COLTS, CALVES AND OTHER CALAMITIES

When the cloud of dust from the little dirt road leading to our end of town signaled the arrival of friends or visitors we'd drop paste or paint brush, hammer or saw, bridle or branding iron and take off, for "All work and no play makes progress," but that was far from our first and only priority.

They came from near and far, family, dear ones, acquaintances and even strangers but they remained strangers only as long as it took to get the coffeepot and cups on the table. Many of Nellie's choicest stories came from people who had stayed at the Palace Hotel years ago and had returned out of curiosity. They were delighted with the restoration and enchanted by Nellie's charm and hospitality.

Some of the happiest of all occasions, of course, were the frequent visits from the family. The Haentjens, Pete, Sally and Peetie were favorite visitors. During that first memorable family reunion, Pete had noticed a most remarkable improvement in his physical well-being. In cold, damp Pennsylavania he suffered from muscle cramps in both legs and Berger's Disease was suspected. The dry, hot climate in the southwest alleviated his pains more successfully than all the painkillers his money could buy.

Pete's firm, the Barrett and Haentjens Pump company, a family company, needed to expand their operations to supply the mines in the western part of the country, including Canada and Mexico. It was agreed that Pete was the logical one of the family to go west. Rock House and the Bar T H Ranch became Pete's headquarters until a suitable business location could be found. With methodical thoroughness, Pete charted the mines, and their potential sites, then chose a location central to his prospective customers. Phoenix, Arizona would become Sally and Pete's new office and home.

Whenever possible, Sally accompanied Pete on his travels and left Peetie with us. He became my third child and I adored him. Occasionally, however, his childish exuberance nearly caused me to have a heart attack from fright.

One afternoon, as he came down the steps after his nap, his childish voice let out a scream. "Maggie! Maggie! A snake! Maggie, it's a great big snake!" He sounded terrified.

And it was a great big snake stretched full-length across the step just below him. Fortunately, he'd seen it and had stopped to scream for help before he stepped on it but he was too frightened to retreat.

"Go back to the top of the stairs, Peetie." I commanded much more calmly than I felt. "I don't think it's a rattlesnake but I can't be sure. You watch the snake and if it moves tell me where it's gone. I'll get Henry."

Thank heavens, Henry was home, working on his new cedar post corral. His short-legged choppy run brought him in record time to my yell of "rattlesnake!" The snake had not moved a muscle.

"Aw hell, Maggie. That's nothing but a sleepy old bull snake." He was cleary disgusted.

I was relieved. "But the darn things look so much alike and they can scare you just as bad," I defended myself.

He chuckled. "Yeah! I guess you're right. I've had a few of them give me quite a start. But bull snakes are very useful and I'm not about to kill this one. But do you want to see how I would kill it if it was a rattlesnake?"

"Do I have to? I hate snakes, even the good ones," I answered.

"Well, I've got to get him outside and this is the best way I know. It's a pretty good trick. Peetie, you can come down now. It's not a rattler, it's a friendly snake. I'm mighty proud of you for calling Maggie. Any time you see a snake, you call for help, OK?"

He quickly but firmly placed his booted foot just behind the snake's head so it couldn't wiggle away. "I couldn't take a chance like this with a rattlesnake as he'd be coiled and ready to strike so I'd have to find a forked branch or a tool or something to pin his head down. Now with my left hand, I hold the snake just behind the boney structure of his head."

He reached down to grasp the snake. By now the sleepy snake was a mass of writhing muscles and hissing in righteous protest. Peetie was only a few steps above and watching every moment with fascination. I was below and wishing I was somewhere else.

"If you get a big *bravo* rattler, here's where you gotta be careful." Henry instructed. "I had a big, strong one twist around my arm and I had to let go of his head and shake him off but he was so anxious to get away he didn't stop to strike me and I was so glad that I just let him go.

"Now I take my right hand and follow it down the length of

his body, holding it so tight it can't wiggle anymore. Come on. We gotta finish this outside."

We marched out with Henry who was holding the snake as rigid as an extra long yardstick. The poor thing had even stopped hissing.

"Now to kill him," Henry continued, "I'd get both arms going like so." He started to swing both arms in a circular motion above his head. "Then I'd let go it's head and pop the snake like a bull whip. It's head would snap off and land a good distance away. But since we don't want to kill this one we'll just turn him loose." Henry slowed, then stopped his circular arm motions, walked over to the protection of the lilac trees, stooped and let his captive slither away. The poor thing must have told his friends that old Rock House was a very frightening place, for we never saw another bull snake in the house.

Not long after that, Peetie did not answer my call. (He was not aware of the consequences of not answering my whistle.) I called, I searched and even Henry became alarmed and joined me. Professor, his inseparable boxer, was not to be found, either.

"Henry, do you think Peetie was missing his Mom and Dad so much that he's run away to try to find them?"

"No. That's the last thing I'm worried about. He loves you and all of us dearly and is as happy as a lark out here. There is something that is bothering me, though. Come on." Henry was very concerned.

We were getting in the car and he continued, "You know how fascinated that kid is with trains. Well, it's about time for the Super Chief to come roaring through and I wouldn't put it past him to try to find a better spot to see it than by running along beside it here in Cerrillos."

"Oh my God! No!" I prayed.

"And I think I know where the spot is. At least I hope so. He's not a dumb kid." Henry said.

He made a fast beeline for the railroad overpass. As we topped the incline, there was Peetie and his dog, waiting for the mightiest of them all, its distant whistle announcing its thunderous arrival. He was leaning far beyond the point of safety over the guardrail. A gust of wind could have blown him in the path of that onrushing train. I suppressed a scream as Henry grasped my knee.

"For the Lord's sake, don't startle him. He'll fall over for

sure." Henry commanded.

He rolled to a stop on the opposite side of the road, turned off the motor as we quietly got out. Peetie remained oblivious to everything on earth but his beloved train. We silently crossed the road and were within clutching distance before speaking to him. He treated our arrival as if he was expecting us. I knew I could not handle the situation so I gave Henry a nod.

Before Henry could wind himself up for a lecture or scolding, the Super Chief flashed by. The expression on the boy's face was ecstatic.

"I can see him better from here," was his innocent explanation.

A scolding? Henry took his hand to cross the road and simply said, "Peetie, this is a pretty dangerous road for you and Professor to be walking alone. Lots of crazy drivers out here. I think you'd better watch your trains from the house."

Peetie obeyed and was never on the road alone again.

An incident that frightened all of us beyond the power of speech, literally, happened the following summer. Peetie had been told never to go in the corral alone if there was any livestock in it. Henry had brought in a small herd of mares and their colts to be branded and cut. Either Peetie did not consider horses livestock or his love of them prompted him to disobey Henry's orders. I glanced out the kitchen door and to my horror, Peetie was alone in the lot with the half-wild mares and totally wild colts.

"Henry!" I gasped and pointed.

He was out of his chair as if he'd sat on a hot coal and to the kitchen door when he stopped as abruptly as he'd started. I was hot on his heels and almost knocked us both down as I bumped into him.

"For the Lord's sake, Henry!" I could not see beyond him.

"Don't utter a sound, Maggie. Just pray if you still know how to." He whispered.

He stepped aside. Peetie had gone up to the largest colt that was standing still and had thrown both arms around his hind legs in a bear hug of true love. How easily that wild young animal could have raised both legs in a vicious kick that could have sent the child into the world beyond.

I grasped Henry's arm and moaned "Oh my God!"

"Not a sound, Maggie. Just pray!" He admonished.

Either my prayer was heard or the colt was itself too frightened to move, or perhaps he was not frightened at all. He stood as motionless as we were. Before long, Peetie's chubby little arms tired so he kissed the colt's leg, loosened his hug and walked away. He looked as satisfied as if he'd just kissed his Mommie. This time Henry was very firm with his scolding. After that, Peetie never went in the lot alone again if there was an aminal in it.

Glenda did not get off so easily when she tangled with a wild ranch animal. About dusk one evening she came running in the kitchen with a desperate plea in both voice and eyes.

"Mother! Mother! I've got to have some help! I know you're busy getting supper but you'll have to stop and help me. I need you!"

"What's so important that it can't wait till after supper. It doesn't do a thing for food to get half-cooked, cold, then cooked again." I protested.

"No, Mother. It can't wait. It'll be dark and Henry'll be home and I have to have your help. Right now!" Her desperation was real.

It should have been. She had disobeyed one of Henry's strictest orders, "Glenda, you can rope Pot or the neighbors' kids or the fence posts, but don't, and I do mean *do not* let me catch you roping one of the calves or colts or any livestock in the lot ever! Do you understand?"

"Yes. I understand, Henry." She replied meekly.

She always obeyed in voice and manner only. Then she did exactly as she pleased.

Not only had she roped a calf, it was a half-grown Brahman calf and in the same lot with its indignant, ferocious mama. Glenda's education had not yet included the knowledge of the natural protective instincts of a mother. Every time she climbed off the wooden gate to try to get the catch off the young calf's neck, Mama Brahman made a determined move toward her and twice Glenda had escaped her razor sharp horns by a matter of inches. Yes! She did indeed need help and a whole lot more than I could give.

"And just exactly what do you expect me to do, Missy?" I was so exasperated with her I could have turned her upside down then and there and given her a good spanking. Then I decided Henry could and would do a much better job than I.

113

"Mommie, can't you go down to the other gate on the far end of this lot and get her to chase you? Be sure to stay close to the gate though so you can climb it if you have to. While she's chasing you, I can get the rope off the calf."

That was an excellent plan, as far as she was concerned, but *not* for me! "Not on your life — or mine, young lady. You got yourself in this mess. You know how Henry feels about your roping his livestock and you have deliberately disobeyed him. Even if you can get the rope off, you are going to have to tell him, or shall I?"

"Oh Mother! You wouldn't do that to me!" She pleaded. "He'll be furious with me!"

"No more so than you deserve!" I said. Suffering from her own mistakes was the only way discipline ever sunk into her Taurus stubborness. "No way am I going to help you out of this one even if I could!"

I was about to turn on my heels and return to supper when she tried once more to get out of her predicament without my help. The cow did not wait till Glenda reached the ground. She charged the gate, just missing her. My heart flew to my throat. No telling what this crazy kid would do in her desperation.

"Glenda, you have no choice." I said very firmly. "You will have to wait till Henry gets home. Come to the house with me."

"She didn't budge. "But Mother, it'll get dark. What'll I do then?"

"You'll have to resort to lanterns and a flashlight. Come! Now!" I commanded.

Henry finally got home. The words tumbled out of Glenda's quivering little mouth in confusion as she made her confession as rapidly as possible. It was then that I could appreciate her apprehension. Henry was furious, shaking chin and all! I did not return to the lot with them. Henry did not spank her. She wished he had. His stern lecture was far worse. I could see where tears had washed a clean path down her chubby little cheeks.

Several days later I had occasion to go to one of the rooms in the old adobe wing and glance out toward the corral. Glenda was diligently practicing roping on the jagged cedar posts. About every third loop fell where it was aimed. I was proud of her.

Then I noticed Henry returning by horseback across the flat above the Galisteo River. When he got close enough to see that Glenda was practicing roping he stopped and silently watched her for a long time. When he got to the corral, he dismounted, ignored his tired horse and immediately started helping her, first by taking the rope and showing her, then by holding her wrist and hand and helping her. The improvement was instant and remarkable. She was not tear stained when she returned from roping this time. There was a happy sparkle in her eyes.

"Henry loves me again, Mommie." She beamed. "He's teaching me how to rope."

CHAPTER 14
THE WILD MARES

My father's three brothers had large ranch holdings in the Tucumcari country. Their combined acreage ran into the hundreds of thousands and made Hnery's ranch look like a corner lot in comparison. Their livestock was also counted in the thousands and they had so many horses that it was impossible to brand, break and ride them all. If they were allowed to run wild too long they became "outlaws" and too unmanageable to be used as saddle horses. Aunt Bess Trigg had just such a problem and put in a call for Henry. He was jubilant when he returned from the Zucal's phone.

"Maggie, that was Aunt Bess. She has eight mares she wants to *give* me. They're too old and wild to break for saddle horses but they are excellent brood mares and I shore need some new colts. We gotta go and get them."

"When?" I asked. "And how are you going to get them back here?"

"Just as soon as we can get off," he replied. "I don't have time to find a truck to borrow or rent so we'll have to take Ray with us to drive them back. He is one of the best horesemen in this part of the country, if not *the* best and I can trust him to get them home."

Henry's "we" was never a casual invitation. It meant I was needed and participation was not voluntary. Ray, an Indian from the Zia Pueblo was working for Henry and it would just be part of his job. It was December and bone-chilling cold. I had already begun to consider the rigors of the couple of hundred miles between Rock House and the Trigg Ranch.

"It's near freezing, Henry." I complained. "My car is in the shop and I am not driving over there in that darned old Jeep!"

"Guess we'll have to take Mother's LaSalle then." He reasoned.

"Rats!" I protested. "It was made before the advent of heaters plus I just don't trust it anymore."

"No choice, Maggie. But don't worry. I just had a complete checkup on her and she'll get us there okay. Wear your warmest clothes and pack your toothbrush and a change of clothes. We'll be gone a couple of days. The ranch is only about fifty miles beyond Tucumcari and we should be there by supper time."

It was a typical cold but crystal clear December day and there was no reason to think of snow chains. So naturally, about forty miles before we got to Tucumcari we ran into a blinding snowstorm. It was early afternoon but the world had turned as dark as sundown. I flipped on the lights then the windshield wipers. Not one flutter or shudder. I flipped and flipped again. They were dead!

"Damn it! I thought you said a *complete* checkup, Henry."

"Hell! I thought so too, Maggie, but I guess it was just a case of 'you don't need a windshield on such a sunny day'!"

"Well, in this case you can drive. It's your turn anyway."

"You gotta keep on driving, Maggie. We can't afford to stop. We don't have any chains and we can't lose momentum or we'll get stuck and be marooned out here all night." Henry's tone was concerned.

He was right. We hadn't seen a car for miles, coming or going. It was like driving with a sheet of paper slapped against the windshield. I hated driving in the snow under any conditions but this was just too much!

"Just how am I going to see? Are you going to sit on the hood and push the wiper?" I growled.

"All right, wise guy." He answered. "All you have to do is keep your foot on the gas pedal and I'll tell you how fast or slow to drive and what to do with the steering wheel."

"Oh! Is *that* all?" I couldn't resist retorting.

"Keep a steady speed and don't let your wheels start spinning. Don't shift gears unless you have to." Henry took command. "Ray, open the window from the left side and guide her. I'll take the right side. The snow on the pavement isn't too heavy yet so the road should feel pretty solid. If you get into anything soft, you're off the road so turn the other way. But don't turn your wheels too sharp or you'll start skidding."

Great! Just great! Oh, for sunny, southern California! I thought. We were getting into the rough country; hills, curves and drop-offs of many hundreds of feet without a guardrail on either side. I drove just fast enough to keep the wheels turning and slow enough to brake if I missed a turn and seemed headed for a bottomless ravine.

"A little to the left. No, not quite so fast! Okay for a minute. Hold it steady. A curve to the left in about twenty feet. There's a pretty steep hill coming so give her a little more gas. Another curve coming up on the right. Not so much gas, it's a down grade." Both windows were open and I was caught in a murderous cross draft, of words and air.

I don't think I was praying, I was too busy concentrating on just keeping us alive, but a miracle did happen. A big truck came lumbering up behind us, the first vehicle we'd seen in hours, and the driver must have observed that we were having trouble and that we had no windshield wipers. He blinked his lights to pass then blinked them again to indicate that I was to follow him. He was making hard snow tracks for us and going slow enough for me to keep behind him. We followed that heaven-sent truck the remaining miles into Tucumcari in relative safety and sanity.

It seemed like midnight before I saw the first fuzzy lights in the outskirts of Tucumcari. The old Concho Hotel was as welcome as a palace and a steaming hot bath gradually thawed the half-frozen marrow of my bones. After supper, that crazy brother of mine and Ray wanted to go to a movie. I couldn't tell them not to go but I sure wasn't going to join them.

I was almost sound asleep when a horn started honking. It didn't stop. It couldn't stop. It was stuck. I sat up in bed with a jolt. There was only one horn in the whole world that sounded like that and it was locked in the bowels of Nellie's LaSalle! The hood could be opened only by pulling a lever inside the car.

I jerked on my clothes and started frantically searching for the keys. Then I remembered I had given them to Henry just in case! Now what! I wouldn't have any trouble finding the car but *where* was the blasted theater?

I didn't wait for the elevator but the night clerk was waiting for me. With a knowing smirk he said, "The movie is two blocks down the street on the other side. You can't miss it."

As I raced down the street, I glanced back at the hotel. Lights were popping on in many of the rooms. I wondered if everybody in Tucumcari was awake by now. I startled a dozing boy in the box office half out of his senses. I was sure he was the only one in town still asleep.

"That God-awful noise! That stuck horn! It belongs to two guys in there. I gotta find 'em!" I didn't wait for him to give me permission to crash the gate and I didn't have any trouble finding the "two guys." Who in his right mind would be out on a night like this? They were among six other "crazies."

"Hurry! Hurry up, you two. That horn has been blasting like that for half an hour!" I blurted out.

"What's the hurry then?" Henry drawled. "Everybody's already awake that's gonna wake up and the others aren't gonna wake up anyway." I could have choked him.

Just as we got to the car the wires burned out. Blissful silence at last. It never honked again. Without a horn the car was useless as far as Nellie was concerned. She bought a new Pontiac the following month.

Early next morning, Henry slipped, slithered, and slid through snow, ice and mud to the Trigg Ranch but not before we got the windshield wipers fixed. I had refused to budge an inch if they weren't fixed. I didn't have to stomp my feet or have a temper tantrum; I just gave Henry the "whammy look" (as the kids called it) and he headed for the first garage. It snowed off and on all day and by noon we were at the ranch. It was a special joy to see Aunt Bess and to return to the warmth and hospitality of that lovely, rambling old house again. The agonies of the previous day were forgotten as soon as I saw the expression of happiness on Henry's face when we went to the corral to see the mares.

"Gee, Aunt Bess, these are the prettiest mares I've seen in a long time. Are you sure you want to give them to me? Can't I pay you something for them?"

"No Henry, but thanks for offering. We have too many and I'm afraid these have run wild so long they are going to be hard to handle." Aunt Bess replied in her gentle Southern drawl. "It is such a raw cold day, wait till tomorrow to brand them. The storm should be over tonight."

"Sure, Aunt Bess. It will give us time to sit and visit. Maybe by tomorrow they'll be a little less skittish. They don't act like they enjoy being behind this high fence." Henry said.

"Can't you wait until you get home to brand them, Henry?" I asked.

"Nope. Wish I could but the branding inspector and state law says they have to have my brand on them before they can be moved anywhere." Henry answered.

Aunt Bess's weather forecast had been correct. A brilliant sun burst out of a gem-like sky reflecting a world of glimmering diamonds and white Christmas trees as far as the eye could see. The crunch of snow was like walking on ground glass. But Henry's hope that the mares would be less skittish was exactly wrong. Being penned up another night had only added to their anxieties and each one was a separate generator, sparking electric charges of apprehension and fear that bounced from one to the other. On the highest, driest ground the branding fire was lighted and the irons put in to heat. I ran the branding irons.

Henry and Ray uncoiled their ropes, stretched and limbered them up and threw a few practice loops. The sight of men and ropes in the corral sent the mares into terrified frenzy. They had an uncanny ability to dodge a loop and they bunched in a herd so an exposed head was a rarity. But once a loop tightened around a neck, a charge of dynamite exploded. It took Henry and Ray and two of Aunt Bess's top cowhands to tie and hold them for the searing branding iron.

Normally, branding eight animals was an hour job, two if you were short on help. Not until sundown did the last mare wear the Bar T H brand. After hot baths and a hearty country supper, maps were brought out. Land grant maps, road maps, any and all available maps were spread on the table and Ray's overland route back to the Bar T H was carefully plotted. It should take him four days, five if he had any trouble, to get back home. We finished off the evening around a slowly dying bed of embers from pungent cedar, with some of Aunt Bess's finest imported cognac.

By daybreak we'd had breakfast, said our good-bys and were on our way, Henry driving the LaSalle; Ray herding eight of the wildest, orneriest animals I'd ever seen. Henry and I were back at Rock House by midafternoon. Ray was expected before the end of the week. Two days later we had a pasture ready for the mares so we could keep them from joining our own "outlaws," never to be seen again.

By the end of the fifth day we began to get a little apprehensive when Ray didn't appear. After a week we were downright worried. By the ninth day Henry was preparing to send out a search party fo Ray and the mares. Midmorning of the tenth day an exhausted Ray brought the still fresh mares into Henry's corrals. I guess they had taken the "scenic route" as Ray had chased them half way across the state of New Mexico.

Henry kept the mares in the trap pasture for a long time, trying to gentle them by feeding them hay, walking and riding among them and talking to them. He longed to turn them out but he still had too many wild horses running on the ranch and he'd have to wait till the weather warmed up before he could organize another broomie chase.

When spring had finally thawed enough snow so that we could round up the wild horses, I was "allowed" to join the professionals. "I shoulda stood in bed!" as Pete would have said. I was assigned the Sierra Gato (Cat Range), the highest, roughest, meanest ridge on Henry's ranch, and Jake to ride, his biggest, roughest, toughest horse. Henry and I trotted up the trail adjacent to the highway to the summit of this treacherous, stony ridge.

"Ride this ridge out, Maggie then head down toward camp. That's where we're going to try to trap the wild ones. Just give Jake his head and let him pick his own way. He knows the loose rocks and safe spots a lot better'n you do. He'll also let you know if there is a wild horse within half a mile."

"How?" I interrupted.

"He'll nicker at them, Dummy. Keep your eyes peeled and your ears alert for anything that moves. I'm going on up into the Ortiz Mountain. Adios." Off he trotted.

As I turned off the trail and started across the ridge, Jake slowed to a walk. The ridge was narrow and fairly flat but the ground was strewn with boulders from medium to monolith size and Jake twisted and turned his way among them. I reached down and patted his shoulder. "I won't have to suffer your hard trot today ol' boy."

I was enthralled with the spectacular vista that fanned out below me from the Ortiz Mountain to Sandia, then across to the Jemez Range and on to the Sangre de Cristo Mountains and miles and miles of plain land that dissolved into the sky. It was early spring and a more magnificent day had never dawned. The world radiated every earth tone of color that nature could create. It was utterly breathtaking and I felt as if I was suspended in space and time stood absolutely still.

Jake stopped. In front of us was an abyss; the ridge plunged down in treacherous descent. Jake's ears shifted forward and backward, the backward as if awaiting my command, the forward as if trying to discern the safest path down that near-cliff. Henry had sent me to this pinnacle to "keep my eyes peeled and ears alert" so we sat very quietly for a long time. We didn't see anything moving so I tightened my knees against Jake's sides and said, "Come on ol' boy. We gotta go down and I'm countin' on you!"

I kept a light but firm pressure on the reins with one hand and firmly clutched the saddle horn with the other, and tried to convince myself that I wasn't in a state of panic. It seemed to take

forever to snake our way down that mountain side but Jake was so careful, so sure-footed I almost regained my self-confidence. When we finally reached the gentle sloping valley it seemed like a bridle path by comparison.

My riding days had been few and far between and next morning I was in agony! My muscles were not attuned to those grueling mountainous miles and each and every one was writhing in protest! How could I possibly get one foot in a stirrup and the other over the saddle for today's ride. But I had "signed up." I had to go. After about half an hour, the aching muscles relaxed and the pain gradually went away. I did not have to return to that dreaded Sierra Gato and Jake, lucky horse, had been turned out to pasture, his day's work was done. White Man was my mount and the smoother terrain of the west side was my assigned territory.

Getting up the third morning wasn't quite so torturous. Late in the afternoon, I caught my first glimpse of a broomie, but only a glimpse. I knew what Henry meant when he said they moved like a "streak of lightning."

When the last cowpoke had ridden into camp and washed off the dust with well water in the wooden horse trough, we had eight broomies. Not much of a haul for three days riding, but necessary for the safety and integrity of our own saddle horses and the new mares. The best wild ones had been caught on the last chase and Henry did not want to keep any of the eight we had caught this time so he sold or gave them all away. At least his ranch was safe territory for his now not-so-wild Trigg mares and he did get some beautiful colts the next year. I, for one, gave up "broomie chasing" permanently!

CHAPTER 15
TRUCKING

During the forties and fifties, in our part of the world, "commercial cattle trucking" meant anything from uncertainty to unavailability. Finally, thoroughly disgusted with the "Well, I might be able to get to it next week," broken committments, exorbitant rates and downright dishonesty, Henry decided to buy his own rig. After an exhaustive search the selection was a cantankerous 1944 Chevy two-ton cab with a thirty-five foot trailer. It had a total of sixteen forward gears using two shift sticks and overdrive. It had air brakes, enough tires to start a store and more than enough lights to decorate our Christmas tree. It was bright red, and when parked it appeared to take up the entire block in front of the house. Henry was so proud of it he had his Bar T H brand painted in shiny black letters on the red cab door. I admired it, but from a distance!

He had had it about a week when he called me one morning, "Get your hat, Maggie. I need you. Come on."

I never took the time to ask where to or what for. I'd find out soon enough, sometimes too soon. Unfortunately, his malady of falling asleep had not improved with time or age and it was always worse when he was behind the wheel of a vehicle. We climbed in the truck. He maneuvered it skillfully over treacherous Devil's Throne and stopped when we reached level ground. His 'need' for me that day was to teach me to drive that blasted thing so I could go with him on subsequent trips.

"Slip behind the wheel, Maggie. This is as good a place as any to teach you how to handle my truck."

"What, Henry! Did I hear you say you were going to 'teach' me how to handle this!...this...*thing*!! But I *don't want* to...!"

"Don't let your wants hurt you." He interrupted. "Anyway, it's simple once you get the knack of shifting gears. All you gotta remember is you have to double-clutch every time you shift, whether it's an upshift or a downshift. You'll get the hang of it in a few miles."

I was two years his senior and putty in his hands. He showed me the location of the gears, first the right then the left and explained when I should change them. "OK. Let's go."

I put it into low gear, lurched a good many yards like a stiff-legged bronc, then it, or I, settled down. I practiced the next higher gears and always the double-clutch. After a mile or so he said, "OK. You've got it," scrounged down in the seat and promptly went to sleep.

I nudged him awake. "Hey, if you have any idea of waking up where you expect to go, don't you think it would be a good idea to tell me where we're going?"

"Just head for Albuquerque. Gotta pick up a load of hay. But I'll be awake before we get there." He mumbled.

"Drat you, Henry! I could choke you!" I growled. I was wasting my breath. He was sound asleep.

So that's how I became co-chauffeur of a piece of rolling stock that I was mortally afraid of and often loathed and despised. Even so, it did afford moments of entertainment. The first one happened shortly after I was headed west on the two-way highway toward Albuquerque. Henry had scrounged down so low only the top of his head was visible. This was before the advent of 'hippies' and my ear-length hair and bright red lipstick were a dead give away. This could belong only to a female, a thin-faced scrap of a woman, driving this huge thing, apparently all by herself.

A passing driver, wearing an expression of disinterest and boredom, glanced up when he got abreast of me. When he saw that I was a 'dame' he was so astonished he almost ran off the road. When he finally got his car under control, he accelerated as if he thought I intended to pursue him. A few miles farther on, a station wagon loaded with kids passed me and one of them must have remarked that a "little old lady is driving that truck and she's all alone." I almost had to crash-stop to keep from rear-ending the car when the driver slowed down for a "this I gotta see." I was highly amused by the sudden erratic driving patterns of the many vehicles when the drivers chanced to glance at me.

Henry seldom went anywhere in his truck without me. I repected the truck, got pretty good at driving it but my love for it never increased. One time we had to take a maximum load of cattle up to Ignatio, Colorado for summer pasturing. Henry had learned that he had to have a chauffeur's and a trader's license if he was going to truck out of New Mexico. On the way home we stopped in Durango, Colorado to get these papers. Would I also need the special license? "No. Only the owner." No sense in my standing in that stuffy office, waiting for all the red tape. Between the building and the curb where we'd parked was a strip of grass, the greenest, lushest I'd seen since we'd left California. Chiggers or no, I thought. I'm going to sit here and smoke a cigarette.

I smoked the whole thing. Henry didn't return. I stretched out on my side, head propped in my hand, elbow in the grass, watching for any tiny insects. It was warm, the grass was soft and sweet smelling. I put my Stetson hat over my head and went to sleep. No doubt, in my jeans and boots, head covered by the western hat, I looked like any ten or twelve-year old boy.

Eventually Henry got the necessary papers. When his soft-voiced "Maggie" didn't get any response, he gave me a gentle kick across my protruding bottom with the broad side of his boot. As I sat up, I was looking fullface at a man standing on the top of four steps leading from the government building Henry had just left. His expression betrayed his thoughts, My Gawd! That mean old man goes over and kicks that little kid and it turns out to be a woman. I never saw the like! He was so startled he literally stumbled down the first step toward the walk.

As we headed for the truck, Hnery said, "Say Maggie, you've had your nap. How 'bout you driving so I can have mine?"

I crawled up behind the wheel. After I got the motor started and the gears set, I could not resist glancing at my still-staring stranger-friend to see his reaction. His eyes popped and he stumbled down another step. After we turned the corner, I looked back again, gave him my sweetest smile and wickedest wink. Poor man. He missed the next step and almost sprawled on his face. I burst out laughing as we drove out of sight.

"What's so funny, Maggie. Whatcha' laughing at?" Henry asked.

I repeated the incident. "Aw Maggie! Aren't you ever going to grow up?" He chuckled.

"Not if I can help it." I grinned back.

A few weeks later we had our second herd of cattle rounded up, loaded up and were heading for the greener grasses of Colorado. This trip we were being followed in a pickup truck by "Bugger" Coleman, cousin of the owner of the ranch where we were going. He knew a great short cut over the Rockie Mountains.

"Cuts off miles and miles, Henry" Bugger had assured us. "May be a little steep but you've got a good truck and we won't have no trouble at all."

Well, we didn't have "no trouble at all" not, that is, until we got within one hundred and fifty feet of the summit of the ten thousand foot pass. With the heat, the weight of twenty-eight head of cattle and the steepness of the last grade up to that elevation, we burned out a main bearing. The truck came to a shuddering halt.

A hasty consultation left but one alternative: Henry and Bugger would leave me with the truck and cattle, they'd return to Espanola in the pickup, rent another cab and hitch it to the trailer. Then they'd tow the broken one to Espanola with the pickup and leave it to be repaired. Bugger could slowly head for Ignatio in the rented cab and loaded trailer.

The familiar butterflies returned to my stomach as I watched them depart. It seemed like a small eternity before the tiny black dot disappeared miles and miles and miles down the mountain side.

We were close enough to the summit so that I could see the valley in front of me stretching out in both directions for Lord knows how many miles. It could have been hundreds! I felt like an infinitesimal grain of sand in that vast loneliness; not a soul, not even one vehicle coming or going on that endless road; not a sound except for an occasional bawl of protest from the caged animals behind me. It was a breathtaking sight. I let my mind and soul soak up its magnificent splendor. Very gradually it became an awesome one, then ominous! Two storms were gathering, one at either end of that vast wilderness, picking up momentum and fury in their angry rush to clash head on somewhere in the endless distance.

The cattle instinctively sensed the approach of that terrible conflict of elements. They became restless, their bawls louder, more frequent and contagious. The storms sped towards us. Darts of lightning dashed earthward with a pistol-shot concussion upon contact with the earth, then deafening roars of thunder. The animals' anxiety reached stampede proportions; the trailer was shaking like a paper sack. It woudn't have surprised me if they had turned it completely over in their fear-crazed desire for freedom. I forced myself to leave the security of the cab and look at the poor imprisoned creatures. My heart contracted like a tight fist, then almost stopped. I screamed into the howl of the storm "Oh dear God! Oh no! Oh no!"

One terrified beast had attempted to climb the wood slats of the siding to gain her freedom. Her left leg was wedged between the slats almost at the top, trapped beneath her thrashing body. Adding to this horror, another cow had managed to climb her way over the beast's trapped leg and could move neither forward or backward and was suspended in mid air. I had to swallow hard and breathe deeply to keep from being violently ill.

A sense of utter hopelessness engulfed me. In all my life, I had never felt so inadequate. I glared at the approacing storms, about equally distant from the summit where we were stranded and now where they would obviously collide with a violence beyond belief.

Was there no way I could alleviate the suffering of these poor, wretched animals? Was there no human being in this infinity of wind, lightning and thunder? I searched the road in each direction, hoping, praying. From the direction where Henry had disappeared eons ago, a tiny black spot gradually emerged into my range of vision. It was so small it could be some terrified animal. Without hope, I watched the spot; I could not take my eyes away from it. It did not disappear; it grew larger and larger until finally I could tell that it was a motorcycle, speeding beyond safety into the killing storm, with two people on it.

"Oh merciful God, please let them have some means of helping me liberate these poor cows!" I prayed aloud.

Miles and miles before they reached me, I was standing in the middle of the road, frantically waving my arms like an animated scarecrow, oblivious to the quarter-size raindrops that were splashing patterns on the dust covered road. The motorcycle stopped. The two men who jumped off could not conceal their astonishment at finding a lone female and a very distraught one at that.

"Lady, what's the matter? What can we do to help?" One of them asked.

Words would not come through my constricted throat. I dumbly pointed toward the trailer.

"My Gawd!" Exclaimed the other young man. "And you here all alone! How'n hell did you get yourself in *this* mess?"

Raindrops were spattering down, bigger and faster. I had not time for a lengthy explanation. "We broke down. My brother's gone for help." I stammered.

They were so astonished at seeing me that they had not fully observed the plight of the poor beasts trapped in the trailer. "My God!" cried the first fellow. "I never saw the likes of that before!"

"And I hope I never do again!" added the other. "We gotta do something! But what!"

Three blank faces stared one to the other. The noise of the

storm had grown so intense we had to shout to be heard. "Say, Jake, did you bring your hatchet?"

"Hatchet! Oh no!" I hollered. "You *can't* cut her foot off!"

"No Ma'am. Wasn't aimin' to. Just goin' to hack the slat out around her foot. As least that'll let the other cow get off of her."

The fury of the storm lent speed to their chopping and well placed blows soon brought release for the brutally torn hoof.

"Ma'am, anything else we can do?"

"Nothing you can do." I said hopelessly. "Thank you anyway, but I don't think there is a thing any of us can do. But please, you're heading directly into that storm. Park your motorcycle under the truck and sit in the cab until the worst is over. Only God knows how bad the middle of the storm will be." The rain drops were getting smaller but increasing in intensity.

"No. No thank you Ma'am. We're used to these storms. We've been in them before. Got a long way to go and we hate to leave you here alone but you'll be OK. Just stay in the cab when the lightning gets really bad. We'll be on our way if we can't help you no more."

"No. There's nothing more you can do and I'll never be able to thank you for what you've already done. I wish you'd stay. If you can't, please drive carefully and 'Vaya con Dios!' Go with God!"

The roar of thunder drowned out the roar of their motor. Rapidly they disappeared below and behind a wall of clouds. I've often wondered how they made it.

The last tiny patch of sky vanished behind the churning smoke-colored clouds as those gigantic storms pitted their strength one against the other. A multi-pronged streak of lightning struck a tall, proud pine tree not fifty yards away like a burst of mortar fire. I raced for the security of the cab. The angry clouds gave vent to rain; not drops, not sheets, but a solid wall of water. I could not see the front end of the truck, a mere four feet in front of me; the windshield could have been made of opaque glass. The rain, now laced with hail was surely pounding its way through the roof of the cab. I was alone and afraid. I felt that death was very near.

How long it took for the storm to rage across the summit and down through the opposite valley, I'll never know. My searching eyes were sore and stinging when I finally spotted the approaching dots that were the pickup and cab many miles below. The rain was slowly tapering off.

However, the storm was but a forerunner of woes yet to come! Upon his arrival, Henry had given me a piercing look and asked if I was okay. I nodded weakly. He neither wanted or needed a lengthy answer. I had survived. That was enough.

The only cab that could be rented in the sleepy little village was about six inches higher than the hitch of Hnery's trailer. Loaded as it was, the trailer couldn't possibly be raised and hooked onto the cab, the cab would have to be lowered! Digging through that resurfaced road was difficult. We finally got the rented cab hitched to the trailer and Henry's cab hitched to the pickup with a log chain.

I was opening the door of the rented cab, expecting a long wait until they returned again from Espanola when Henry called, "No, Maggie. You get in my cab. Bugger is going to drive on slowly with the cattle and I'll catch up with him later. I want to tow my cab to Espanola. You'll have to steer it."

Drat that brother of mine! Choking was too gentle! I believed in the old proverb: "The Lord gives you only the burdens you have the strength to bear." But just how strong did Henry think I was? His motto was: "Where there is a will there is a way." He took it for granted that my "strength" would be equal to his "will and way."

As I crawled into the driver's side of that hateful red truck, Henry said, "Maggie, this may be kinda tricky for you." (What an understatement!) "You can't turn on the motor 'cause it'll burn the whole truck up for sure. So you'll have to coast down. Use your brakes as little as possible. I'll watch you and keep ahead of you but you be careful not to rear-end me." He jumped in the pickup and we were on our way before I could utter a groan of protest. It would have been wasted anyway.

Five thousand feet on a treacherous, slippery mountain road! In a "dead" truck! TERRIFIC!!! He had to be out of his mind!

The first hour presented few problems. The storm, with a head start, was many miles down the valley before we caught up with its ragtag remnants. Oh dear Lord, I thought, not that wall of water again! As we neared civilization, the globs of mud from the dust encrusted highway were spewed on my windshield from the back of the pickup in front of me and with the drizzling rain, the visibility varied between poor and none. My nerves were like high-tension wires. Houses began to appear through a drizzle of mud. A ray of hope! We should be there pretty soon.

Then all hell broke loose! Without warning, Henry hit a deep dip. It was semi-liquid mud and it totally covered my windshield. At the same moment, an oncoming car splashed me from the other side. I was enclosed in a mud box. I could not see a thing! There was no time to turn the windshield wipers on but I did put slight pressure on the brakes. Then I felt a mighty jerk. Henry had to gun the pickup to avoid a rear end crash. I lurched blindly forward and the right front wheel ran over the tow chain. Only Henry's masterly maneuvering saved us both from a horrible smashup. My mixed emotions ranged from sheer terror at the situation to anger that Henry had involved me in this horrible mess to concern that he would be angry that I hadn't done the job right.

When we finally made it to the garage, he was positively apologetic. "I didn't see that dip, Maggie. Sorry. It sure wasn't your fault, you did a good job."

I was so exhausted I longed to stretch out in the back of the pickup and sleep all the way to Ignatio. No such luck!

"Got any money, Maggie?" Henry asked. He never did, only a checkbook. I had soon learned that it was a matter of survival to alway shove a few bucks in my pocket.

"Sure. Want me to get you a cup of coffee or a sandwich or something?"

"No. You're a big girl now and your're on your own. If you think this was bad, its only the beginning and it's gonna get worse. I'm sure you can find a way to get back to Santa Fe and get yourself home. Have you got enough money for a bus ticket?"

Days later, when he finally got home he told us just how much worse it got. "We were through the worst of the storm and late in the afternoon, way down the other side of the valley, we stopped at a ranch to let the cattle out of the trailer. We got most of them out but we had to shoot the cow with the mangled foot and another one with a broken leg. Three got away that we'll never find."

I silently shuddred at the thought of what those few feet to the summit had cost us!!

CHAPTER 16
FINAL DAYS

All the hard work, physical exercise and riding began to take their toll and I found myself in almost constant pain. Aspirin no longer helped and I was unable to conceal my left leg limp from my family. They were insistent that I get some medical treatment and care.

I first went to Lubbock, Texas where I stayed with friends, Shirley and Chris Mansell. Chris was a doctor and it was he who discovered that I had a ruptured disc and a spinal operation was strongly advised.

After much soul searching and tearful consultations with Chris and my family, I decided to have the surgery. I had planned on going to White Memorial Hospital in Temple, Texas where there were still friends of my parents and besides they had been having, according to Chris, great success with spinal operations.

It wasn't too far to Temple. I was still able to drive and had my suitcase packed and was ready to go when I learned that I would have to be in a body cast from chin to knee for at least six months. Furthermore, the bone graft piece would have to be taken from the shin bone so another cast would be accompanied by crutches! No way! I'd just have to find a stronger painkiller.

I returned to Rock House, depressed, miserable and in excruciating pain. I could barely take care of myself, let alone the children or get any productive work done. Nellie turned for help to Dr. Leads, a devoted friend of many years, who had recently moved his practice to Albuquerque. Within a week, Nellie was summoned to the phone.

"Dr. Leads here. How is Margaret Day?" He asked.

"She can't get out of bed except to drag herself to the bathroom." Nellie answered.

"That bad?" He exclaimed. "Well I think I've found just the doctor she's been looking for. Wait right there at the store and I'll phone you back as soon as I can."

Within thirty minutes he called back. At two-thirty that afternoon we were on the way to Albuquerque. At five that evening I was on the operating table. At two in the morning I was in my room with an eight-inch rip down the left side of my spinal column to my left hip bone where splinters had been chipped off to make the bone graft. The ruptured disc, resulting from an old back injury, resembled a shrimp, its tail growing around my left sciatic nerve. Within a short time, I would have been partially or permanently paralyzed. On the eighth day, I was back at Rock House.

The doctor had given me a list of "don't's" before he let me go home.

"You'll be a semi-invalid for about six months," he said.

"Better'n a damn body cast." I couldn't help interrupting.

"And whatever you do, don't fall and break that bone graft. Do you golf?" I shook my head. "Good. You probably never will. Ski?"

"Just fair." I mumbled.

"Give your skis away. I won't ask about horseback riding. That's something you can forget for at least a year, if not forever. And for the rest of your life, don't lift anything that weighs more than twenty pounds."

With such restrictions, I knew there'd be no hope of a successful recuperation at the Bar T H. I agonized. I needed a quieter, gentler place to recuperate but at first, I couldn't face the thought of leaving Mother, Henry and the ranch. Finally I made my decision. Sworn to secrecy, Sally began to look for an unfurnished apartment for the kids and me near her home in Phoenix. It could not be more than I could afford; $125.00 a month at the very most. It was a bombshell when I broke the news to Nellie and Henry. They would not believe me until I started collecting "derelict" pieces of unfinished furniture for my new home.

The next few weeks of preparation and packing were hectic. Nellie and Henry were wonderful, rarely showing any sign of the inevitable sorrow our departure would bring. Even so, as "D Day" drew near the lump in my throat grew proportionately larger.

Finally, the day arrived. The car was loaded and so was the moving van. Henry stalked over to say good-by. His eyes were moist. As he pushed his Stetson back on his forehead, big tears rolled down his cheeks.

"You're making a turrible mistake, Maggie," he turned on his heels and walked away.

Dumb brother, I could have choked him! Instead, I cried all the way to Socorro.

For readers who wonder about that "proverbial" happy ending here are a few facts to serve as an epilogue. Henry got married and he and his wife, Louise, stayed on at the Bar T H. Nellie came to Phoenix to be with me and the kids but Glenda, who had never lost her love for the ranch, spent every summer there. I, too, made many visits back to share in the happy reminiscences and humorous anecdotes of days gone past.